EARLY CIVILIZATION

Jane Chisholm

Anne Millard

Illustrated by **Ian Jackson**

Designed by **Iain Ashman, Radhi Parekh** and **Robert Walster**

History consultant: **George Hart,** British Museum Education Service

Map illustrations by **Robert Walster**

Additional illustrations by **Peter Dennis, Richard Draper, Louise Nixon** and **Gerald Wood**

With thanks to **Lynn Bresler** and **Anthony Marks**

Contents

How to use this book

Dates

Nearly all the dates mentioned in this book are from the period before the birth of Christ. These dates are shown with the letters BC, which stand for 'Before Christ'. Dates in the period after the birth of Christ are indicated by the letters AD, which stand for *Anno Domini* ('Year of our Lord'). To avoid confusion, BC and AD have been used throughout the book. Dates in the BC period are counted backwards from the birth of Christ. For example, the period from 0-99BC is called the first century BC. Periods of a thousand years are counted in *millennia*. The period from 0 to 1000BC is called the first millennium BC.

Many events in ancient history cannot be dated exactly, and so an approximate date is given. Approximate dates are preceded by the letter 'c.', which stands for *circa*, the Latin for 'about'.

Much of the evidence for the dates in this book comes from lists of kings compiled by the Egyptians. These tell us how long a king reigned, who came before and after him, and during which year of the reign an event took place. Experts can then convert these into dates BC.

However some of the lists are incomplete and some experts disagree about how to interpret the available evidence. This means that the dating systems used may vary slightly in some books. This applies particularly to Mesopotamian dates, for which the evidence is especially thin.

About this book

The term civilization is usually applied to a people whose culture has reached a certain stage of development. This stage is characterized by the invention of writing, the use of a calendar, and the development of large social units such as towns and cities, with organized government, law codes and monumental architecture.

This book concentrates on the world's first civilizations which grew up in Egypt and the Middle East in about 3000BC. It also takes a brief look at the earliest cultures of India and China, which developed soon afterwards.

How we know about early civilization

Although early civilization began over 5000 years ago, we have plenty of information about how people lived. Much of it comes from the sources listed below.

Hot, dry climates help to preserve things and a number of stone buildings, such as temples and pyramids, have survived almost intact. These tell us about building technology and styles of architecture. Since the 18th century, archaeologists have excavated a large number of sites, including ancient cities and tombs.

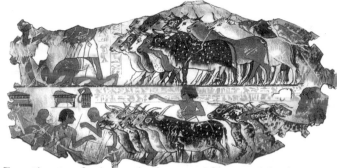

Egyptian tombs in particular provide a wealth of information about daily life and religious beliefs. The interiors were richly decorated with wall-paintings, showing scenes from the person's life and from the lives of the gods. Many of the colours, although faded, are still quite distinct.

In most ancient cultures, people's possessions were buried with them. Furniture, chariots, household items, glass, jewellery and even fragments of clothes and food have all been found preserved in tombs. Also found in tombs are models of people doing things, such as baking bread or herding cattle.

Ancient scripts, such as *hieroglyphics* and *cuneiform* (see pages 10-11), have been found inscribed on buildings and clay tablets, and on scrolls made from a reed called papyrus. For centuries the meaning of these scripts remained a mystery, but since the 19th century scholars have been able to read them. Ancient texts have provided details about a number of things – methods of government, legal systems, the reigns of various rulers, scientific knowledge, religious customs and stories about the gods.

Periods of Egyptian history

For convenience, experts divide Egyptian history into a number of different approximate periods. These are shown in the chart below.

The Predynastic Period c.5000-3100BC

The Archaic Period c.3100-2649BC

The Old Kingdom c.2649-2150BC

The First Intermediate Period c.2150-2040BC

The Middle Kingdom c.2040-1640BC

The Second Intermediate Period c.1640-1552BC

The New Kingdom c.1552-1069BC

The Third Intermediate Period c.1069-664BC

The Late Period c.664-332BC

The Ptolemies c.332-30BC

Unfamilar words

Italic type is used for Egyptian, Greek and Latin words, and for unfamiliar words derived from them. Words followed by a dagger symbol, such as nomad†, are explained in the glossary on page 87. If a person's name is followed by this symbol, you can read more about them in the 'Who's Who' on pages 84-86.

Reference

At the back of the book there is an appendix. This contains a detailed map of Egypt, a list of Egyptian kings, a detailed date chart which outlines the most important events of the period, biographies of rulers and other important people, a glossary and an index.

The beginnings of civilization

The earliest people were nomads† who travelled from place to place, hunting animals and collecting wild plants to eat. Then slowly a more settled way of life developed, based on farming. This transition occurred in different places at different times. It seems to have happened first in about 10,000BC in a part of the Middle East that historians call the Fertile Crescent. This is the area now occupied by Turkey, Syria, Iran and Iraq. Knowledge of farming probably spread as people gradually moved into new areas.

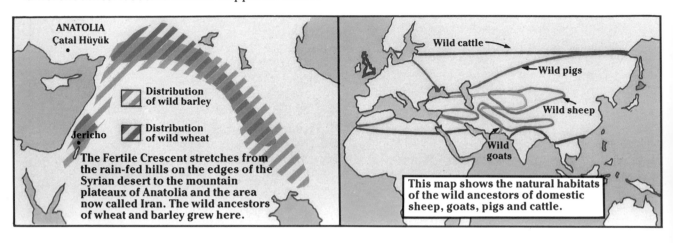

ANATOLIA
Çatal Hüyük

Distribution of wild barley

Distribution of wild wheat

Jericho

The Fertile Crescent stretches from the rain-fed hills on the edges of the Syrian desert to the mountain plateaux of Anatolia and the area now called Iran. The wild ancestors of wheat and barley grew here.

Wild cattle

Wild pigs

Wild sheep

Wild goats

This map shows the natural habitats of the wild ancestors of domestic sheep, goats, pigs and cattle.

The first farmers

The first farmers used sickles to gather grain from edible wild grasses.

Domesticated wheat

Wild wheat

Mutations (natural variations) meant that some ears of grass were less easily scattered by the wind. These were the ones left for people to gather and sow. As a result, more of this type was grown and eventually new domesticated grains evolved.

A large patch of edible wild grasses could provide a group of nomads with food for months. After harvesting, the grasses grew again from seeds sown by the wind, encouraging the group to return to the area year after year. At some point people began to sow the seeds deliberately, to ensure a crop the following year. This committed them to staying in one place in order to tend and harvest the crop.

Hunters began catching very young wild animals to raise themselves. Once tamed, the animals provided a source of milk, wool and meat. The larger, more aggressive, animals were killed off, and slowly, new domesticated strains emerged from the smaller, more docile animals.

Wild sheep

Domestic sheep

The first villages

Once the new farmers had established a settled way of life, they began to build themselves permanent homes from mud and straw. They also developed other new skills to improve their lives.

A reconstruction of an Iraqi hut c.5000BC.

Pottery dates ▲ from c.8000BC. This pot is from Turkey c.5700BC.

Cloth was first spun and woven in about 7000BC. This shows an early Iraqi loom. ▼

This sickle from Çatal Hüyük (see page opposite) is made of ▼ obsidian, a volcanic glass.

Stone vessels were among the earliest inventions. These are ◄ for grinding grain.

The first towns

Nomadic women could only carry one small child each at a time, and so they had to limit the number of children they had, if necessary even by killing unwanted babies. However, once people had settled in villages, they could try to rear all their children and the population began to increase. Some small communities prospered and grew into towns, though little is known about how this way of life developed, as very few towns have been excavated.

Jericho

One of the earliest towns to have been discovered by archaeologists is Jericho, which dates from about 8000BC. Situated near a water source, it appears to have been on an important trade route. Salt and bitumen (tar) from the Dead Sea were probably traded for turquoise, cowrie shells and obsidian (a volcanic glass used for making tools). The people of Jericho grew rich and built walls to protect themselves from envious neighbours.

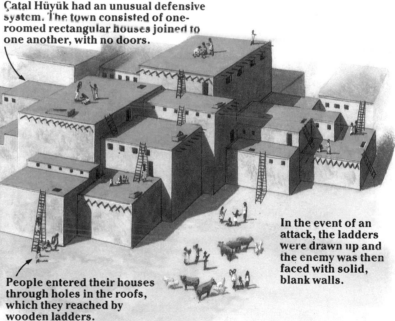

A stone tower, over 9m (29ft) high, has been excavated. There were probably other towers too.

The town was surrounded by a wall over 5m (16ft) high and 1.5m (5ft) wide and a ditch over 8m (27ft) wide and 2m (6ft) deep.

At one time at least 2000 people lived in Jericho in small, round houses made of sunbaked mud-bricks,

Jericho's defences suggest that the town must have had leaders and experts to plan and organize the building work and to provide enough food to feed the workers.

Çatal Hüyük

Another early town has been excavated at Çatal Hüyük in Anatolia. The people there were successful farmers, although trade may have been the source of their wealth. They probably traded cloth and obsidian for shells and useful stones, such as flint. By 6500BC Çatal Hüyük was a flourishing centre. This is a reconstruction of part of the town.

Çatal Hüyük had an unusual defensive system. The town consisted of one-roomed rectangular houses joined to one another, with no doors.

In the event of an attack, the ladders were drawn up and the enemy was then faced with solid, blank walls.

People entered their houses through holes in the roofs, which they reached by wooden ladders.

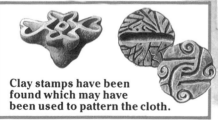

Clay stamps have been found which may have been used to pattern the cloth.

Early religious beliefs

Archaeologists have some idea of the religious beliefs of the people of this period from the number of small carved figures that have been found at ancient sites. Many people seem to have worshipped some form of mother goddess, and sometimes a young god associated with her.

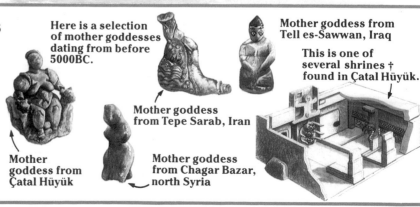

Here is a selection of mother goddesses dating from before 5000BC.

Mother goddess from Tell es-Sawwan, Iraq

This is one of several shrines † found in Çatal Hüyük.

Mother goddess from Tepe Sarab, Iran

Mother goddess from Çatal Hüyük

Mother goddess from Chagar Bazar, north Syria

Sumer

The earliest civilizations all grew up in fertile areas bordering great rivers. One of the first of these was in Mesopotamia (meaning 'between the rivers'), the name given by the Ancient Greeks to the land between the Rivers Tigris and Euphrates. The most dramatic developments took place in the southern part, Sumer, situated in what is now Iraq.

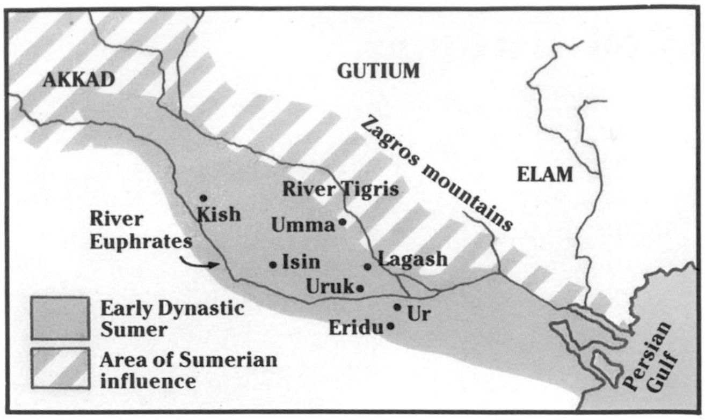

Early Sumer

The map shows:

AKKAD
GUTIUM
Zagros mountains
ELAM
River Tigris
River Euphrates
Kish
Umma
Isin
Uruk
Lagash
Ur
Eridu
Persian Gulf

Early Dynastic Sumer

Area of Sumerian influence

The Sumerians grew wheat, barley, vegetables and dates and reared sheep and cattle.

Fishing, hunting and catching wildfowl provided additional food.

The settlements were clustered on the river banks. The houses were built of sun-dried mud-bricks and there were stables made of matting for the animals.

The farmers built dykes to protect their crops from the flood waters.

A new more efficient plough was introduced in the Uruk period. It was drawn by oxen instead of men, and later had a metal blade. This enabled much larger areas to be ploughed, which increased the crop yield.

Hut for cattle

Potters at work

The potter's wheel was invented in about 3400BC, and later adapted for transport. A donkey pulling a wheeled cart could carry up to three times as much as it could on its back.

The earliest Sumerian culture is called Ubaid, after the site where it was first discovered. By about 5000BC, farmers were established on the river banks and around the marshes. The land was flat and fertile but had little rain, and although the Euphrates flooded its banks each spring, in summer the soil baked hard. Gradually the farmers learned how to build irrigation canals in order to store the water and transfer it to the fields. This allowed more land to be cultivated and the population increased. Surplus food was produced, which allowed some people to become full-time craftsmen, traders or priests, rather than farmers. A few of the larger settlements, such as Eridu, Ur and Uruk, grew into cities and eventually into independent city states†.

In about 4000BC a new phase began, named after Uruk. During this period there was a series of new advances, the most important of which was the invention of writing in about 3000BC (see page 10). The Sumerians also devised an elaborate legal system and became skilled mathematicians and astronomers (see page 64). The reconstruction shown here is of an early Sumerian village.

6

Crafts and trade

The early Sumerians made objects by hammering lumps of copper. In about 4000BC they learned how to produce pure copper from copper ore by heating it at high temperatures. They also discovered how to cast molten (melted) copper, gold and silver in moulds.

In about 3500BC the Sumerians learned how to make bronze, a harder metal, by combining copper and tin. The period from 3000 to 1000BC is often called the Bronze Age, as bronze became so widely used.

Sumerian pots ▲

◄Clay figure

The Sumerians traded agricultural produce, cloth and manufactured goods for timber, stone and metals. Their merchants travelled as far as Anatolia, Armenia, the Mediterranean coast and the Persian Gulf and exchanged goods with Indian traders, at a trading depot such as Dilmun (modern Bahrain).

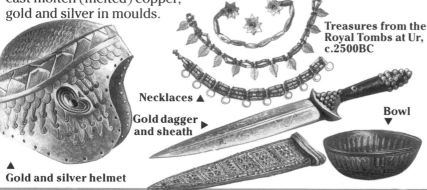

Treasures from the Royal Tombs at Ur, c.2500BC

Necklaces ▲

Gold dagger and sheath ►

Bowl ▼

▲ Gold and silver helmet

Early Sumerian government

At first each city was probably run by a council of elders, although in wartime a leader, or *lugal*, was chosen to direct the campaigns. Wars became increasingly common. There were raids by foreigners and disputes arose between cities whose rulers competed with each other for supremacy. Massive fortifications were built and people came to live in cities for protection.

Battle chariots drawn by wild donkeys, called onagers.

The Early Dynastic Period

As wars became more frequent, *lugals* kept control for longer periods and eventually for life. From about 2900BC *lugals* became kings and founded dynasties† in the most important cities. Later Sumerian lists give details of some of these early kings. They appear to have ruled one after another, although in fact some of them ruled at the same time in different cities.

This decorated relief† (known as the Battle Standard of Ur) shows Sumerian soldiers and chariots in battle.

Dynasty III of Ur

Between about 2400BC and 2100BC Sumer was overrun first by Akkadians (see page 24), then by Gutians, a tribe from the Zagros mountains. In about 2100BC Sumerian supremacy was restored by Ur-Nammu. He founded Dynasty III of Ur and united Sumer under his rule. Later internal rivalries broke out and in about 2000BC Ur was destroyed by Elamites. However Sumerian culture lived on, as it was revived by later rulers of Mesopotamia (see page 24).

Excavations of Dynasty III buildings at Ur show that some wealthy people in towns lived in quite sophisticated houses. The reconstruction below is based on the remains of one of them.

Bedroom

Bedroom

Kitchen

Doors and windows opened on to a central courtyard.

A wooden staircase and balcony gave access to rooms on the first floor.

Sumerian religion

The Sumerians worshipped hundreds of gods and goddesses. They believed that it was important to obey them and make offerings to them. If the gods were angry, they might send punishments such as floods or war. Each city had its own patron deity to look after its interests. There were gods associated with every aspect of life and death. Here are some of the most important ones.

Enki was god of 'sweet waters' and patron of crafts, learning and magic.

Ninhursag was the great mother goddess. She was married to Enlil, god of the air. He took a leading role among the gods and in the affairs of Sumer.

Enlil's son **Nanna** (later renamed Sin) was the moon god.

Nanna's son **Utu** (later Shamash) was the sun god.

Inanna (later Ishtar) was goddess of love and a warrior goddess. She was married to Dumuzi (later called Tammuz).

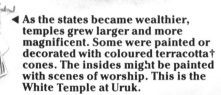

◄ Early temples, like this Ubaid shrine at Eridu, were rectangular mud-brick buildings on low platforms.

◄ As the states became wealthier, temples grew larger and more magnificent. Some were painted or decorated with coloured terracotta† cones. The insides might be painted with scenes of worship. This is the White Temple at Uruk.

Temples

At the centre of each city was a temple to the patron deity. The Sumerians believed the gods owned the city states† and some of the land was worked directly for them by peasants and slaves. The government allotted the rest to temple staff or to farmers who paid part of their crops as rent. Few people owned land outright. Rents, offerings and farm produce were all used to run the temples and to help the poorest citizens. As well as priests and priestesses, each temple employed a large number of officials, scribes†, craftsmen, cooks and cleaners.

◄ New temples were erected on the rubble of the old ones. This raised the platform higher and higher until the ziggurat (temple platform), shown here, became the established style. This reconstruction shows the Dynasty III ziggurat of the moon god of Ur.

Priests and priestesses conducted the rituals.

Musicians and dancers performed at the ceremonies.

Key dates

c.5000BC Ubaid culture: farmers are established in Sumer (southern Mesopotamia).

c.4000BC Uruk culture: the wheel, the ox-drawn plough and writing are invented. The Sumerians discover how to smelt metal.

c.3500 The Sumerians discover how to make bronze.

c.3100-2900BC Jemdet Nasr or proto-literate period: writing is in widespread use.

c.2900-2400BC Early Dynastic Period (Dynasties I and II of Ur): kings are established in leading cities.

c.2400-2100BC Sumer is conquered by Akkadians, and then by Gutians.

c.2100BC Dynasty III: Sumerian power is restored by Ur-Nammu.

Dates for early Mesopotamian history are very approximate, as experts cannot agree on how to interpret the available evidence.

Early Egypt

While city states were developing in Mesopotamia, cultural and economic conditions in Egypt led to the establishment of the world's first great nation. In ancient times Egypt occupied almost the same area as it does today.

The Predynastic Period

The period between about 5000BC and 3100BC is known as the Predynastic Period in Egypt. In the Nile Valley three cultures can be identified that evolved one after the other. They are known as Badarian, Amratian (or Nagada I) and Gerzean (or Nagada II), after the sites where they were first discovered. The people of these cultures made tools, weapons and utensils and were skilled potters and weavers.

Badarian artefacts

Amratian artefacts

Gerzean artefacts

The early Egyptians knew how to control the Nile's annual flood with an elaborate irrigation system (see page 14). They also learned how to work metals, and the use of copper (and later bronze) tools and weapons slowly increased. At first houses were made of mud and reeds, but by Gerzean times these had been replaced by sun-dried mud-brick.

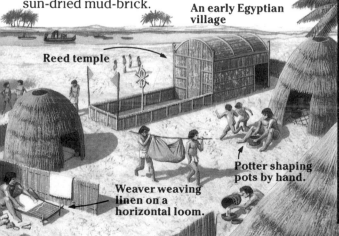

An early Egyptian village

Reed temple

Weaver weaving linen on a horizontal loom.

Potter shaping pots by hand.

Upper and Lower Egypt

By about 3300BC important changes were taking place in southern Egypt which suggest that the population and wealth of the area was growing. Towns were built, defended by high mud-brick walls, and large monuments were constructed as burial places for kings. The art of writing was also discovered at this time (see page 10).

By about 3100BC the communities of the Nile Valley had united into a single kingdom, known as Upper Egypt. The kingdom was ruled from Hierakonpolis by a line of kings who wore white crowns. The kings were buried at a sacred site near Abydos. The Upper Egyptians developed elaborate burial customs, placing personal possessions and offerings in their tombs.

Model animals found in tombs suggest that some creatures had already become linked with certain deities (see page 63).

Very little excavation has taken place in the region of the Nile Delta. However according to Egyptian tradition this area, known as Lower Egypt, had also become one kingdom by this time. Its kings wore red crowns and ruled from Buto. Evidence suggests they had close trading connections with their neighbours in the East.

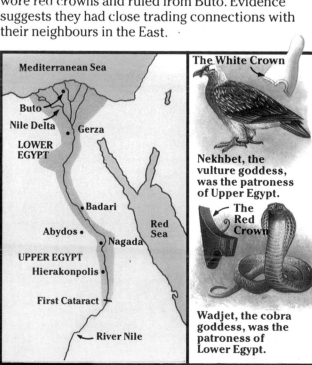

Mediterranean Sea

Buto
Nile Delta
LOWER EGYPT
Gerza

Badari

Abydos •
Nagada

Red Sea

UPPER EGYPT
Hierakonpolis •

First Cataract

River Nile

The White Crown

Nekhbet, the vulture goddess, was the patroness of Upper Egypt.

The Red Crown

Wadjet, the cobra goddess, was the patroness of Lower Egypt.

Writing

The invention of writing is one of the most important landmarks of civilization. It is often said to mark the end of prehistoric times and the beginning of history. This is because writing enabled people to record information accurately, and so helped them to develop a sense of their past.

The first steps towards the development of writing probably took place in Sumer between 4000BC and 3000BC. The new cities were rapidly growing and needed a way of keeping records. Pictograms (simple pictures) were used to indicate objects and quantities, such as the amount of grain or cattle owned by a temple. Later the pictures became more stylized and began to look like symbols.

Cuneiform writing

The first pictograms were drawn in vertical columns with a pen made from a sharpened reed. Then two developments made the process quicker and easier. People began to write in horizontal rows, which avoided smudging. A new type of pen was used which was pushed into the clay, producing 'wedge-shaped' signs that are known as *cuneiform* writing.

Cuneiform writ

Picture writing

Pictograms and *cuneiform* were written on clay tablets, and then baked hard in a kiln.

Egyptian hieroglyphs

In Egypt the first examples of writing appeared between about 3300BC and 3100BC. Some scholars suggest that the Egyptians may have been inspired by seeing the Sumerian script. The Egyptian script is known as *hieroglyphic*, after the Greek for 'holy writing', although the Egyptians themselves called it the 'words of the gods'. To them it had an important religious and magical significance. They believed that the knowledge of writing had been given to them by Thoth, the god of wisdom.

How hieroglyphs work

The Egyptian writing consisted of over 700 signs, or *hieroglyphs*, most of which are recognizable as pictures of things. They probably began by representing objects, and later came to stand for sounds too.

Each hieroglyph corresponded to the sound of one or more letters. For example:

= t   = sw   = n͗h.

At the same time, a sign could also represent an object. For example ⬯ meant mouth, but it also represented the sound 'r' and could be used as part of the word *nfr*, meaning 'beautiful'.

n   f
r

Hieroglyphs normally represented consonants only, though they had a few semi-vowels, such as 'y'. In order to pronounce the language, vowels have to be added and experts sometimes disagree about the correct spellings. For example, the *hieroglyphs* for the name 'imnhtp', can be written as Amenhotep, Amunhotep or Amenhotpe. ▶

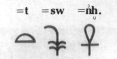

Sometimes a picture representing an object or movement was placed at the end of a word, to clarify its meaning. This is called a determinative.

Determinative for cat

= mjw, meaning 'cat'

Determinative for movement

= tkn, meaning 'to approach'

Hieroglyphs can be written from left to right, right to left, or downwards. If the animals or people are facing left, you read from left to right. If they are facing right, you read from right to left.

These *hieroglyphs* are read from left to right.

These are the same *hieroglyphs*, but read from right to left.

These *hieroglyphs* are read from right to left and down.

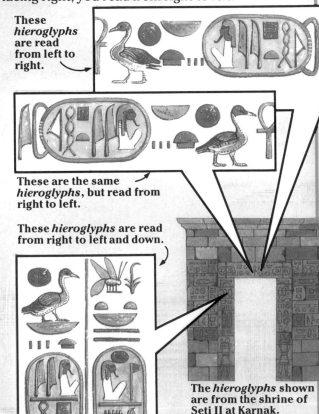

The *hieroglyphs* shown are from the shrine of Seti II at Karnak.

The Egyptian "i" is not like an English "i". It is almost silent, like an intake of breath.

How cuneiform writing developed

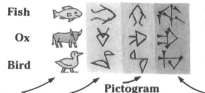

Fish	Ox	Bird

Cuneiform signs bore little resemblance to the original pictures.

Object → Pictogram → **Pictogram turned sideways** → Cuneiform

At first signs were only used to represent objects. Later they began to represent sounds. This meant that abstract concepts could be expressed.

For example, if you used a system of picture writing in English you could write the word 'belief' like this.

Bee   Leaf

Understanding cuneiform

Cuneiform was adapted by the Akkadians, Babylonians and Assyrians to write their own languages and was used in Mesopotamia for about 3000 years.

Knowledge of it was then lost until AD1835, when Henry Rawlinson, an English army officer, found some inscriptions on a cliff at Behistun in Persia. They consisted of identical texts in three languages (Old Persian, Babylonian and Elamite), carved in the reign of King Darius† of Persia (522-486BC). After translating the Persian, Rawlinson began to decipher the others. By 1851 he could read 200 Babylonian signs.

Writing materials

The Egyptians wrote with ink and brushes on papyrus, a paper made from papyrus reeds. They also made notes on pieces of broken pottery or flakes of limestone, known as *ostraca*.

Papyrus scroll   **Palette with ink and brushes**

The ink was made in solid blocks and had to be mixed with water.

Scribes

Early scripts were extremely complicated and years of study were required to learn them properly. People specially trained to read and write were known as scribes. These skills brought them power and status. Scribes could get good jobs in temples or in government and were often exempt from paying taxes.

A statue of an Egyptian scribe

Shorthand scripts

The Egyptians developed two shorthand scripts for daily use. *Hieroglyphs* were kept for religious and state inscriptions.

The first shorthand script is known as *hieratic* and was in use during the Old Kingdom.

During the Late Period (c.700BC), an even more flowing script evolved, which is known as *demotic*.

Deciphering hieroglyphs

The last known example of *hieroglyphs* dates back to AD394. For centuries after that no-one knew how to read them, until 1799 when French soldiers of Napoleon's army unearthed a clue at Rosetta in Egypt. It was a stone slab covered in different kinds of writing – identical texts in *hieroglyphic*, *demotic* and Greek.

The puzzle was finally solved by a French linguist, Jean François Champollion, who published the results of his research in 1822. Champollion deduced that *hieroglyphs* might stand for sounds and letters, rather than objects alone. He built on previous studies which suggested that words inside oval shapes, called cartouches, were the names of rulers.

The Rosetta stone

Champollion first worked out the *hieroglyphs* for Ptolemy, who was mentioned several times in the Greek text.

Ptolemy in *hieroglyphs*

Ptolemy in Greek →

He then went on to construct the name Cleopatra†. The two provided the key from which he was eventually able to work out the other *hieroglyphs*.

11

The Archaic Period and the Old Kingdom

In about 3100BC, a king of Upper Egypt, traditionally known as Menes†, conquered Lower Egypt. He united the two kingdoms under Dynasty I and founded a new capital on the border, at Memphis. Evidence suggests that he married a northern princess, giving their son, Hor-aha, a hereditary claim to the whole of Egypt. The Egyptians never forgot that their country had originally been two lands. The official title of the ruler was 'King of Upper and Lower Egypt'.

This slate carving shows Narmer, an Upper Egyptian king, triumphing over a Lower Egyptian prince. Many believe he and Menes were the same person.

The Archaic Period

The period of the kings of Dynasties I and II is known as the Archaic Period. The kings may have been buried at Sakkara, near Memphis, as their names appear on seals and other objects found there in brick *mastaba* tombs (see page 16). However the same kings' names also appear in tombs in the desert necropolis† at Abydos, where the predynastic kings of Upper Egypt were buried.

This disc was found at Sakkara and dates from about 2950BC.

The Old Kingdom

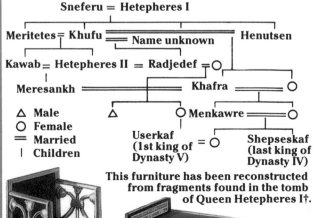

This wall-painting of geese is from a tomb at Meidum, c.2575BC.

The Archaic Period was followed by the Old Kingdom, one of the greatest eras of Egyptian history and culture. It was the age of the pyramids (see page 16). Egypt was united under a strong central government. Trade flourished and Egyptian traders travelled as far afield as Lebanon and Punt (see page 47). The army defended the frontiers and trade routes from Nubians, Libyans and bedouin (desert nomads†). Craftsmen produced fine works of art and scholars standardized writing and the calendar, and studied astronomy, mathematics and medicine.

Imhotep

Imhotep was one of the highest officials of King Zoser† of Dynasty III. He was the architect of the first pyramid, the Step Pyramid of Sakkara (see page 16). He was also a high priest and a doctor and may have had something to do with introducing the calendar. Imhotep's reputation for wisdom was so great that later generations worshipped him as a god. The Ancient Greeks identified him with their god of medicine, Asclepius.

Imhotep

Dynasty IV

These statues show Prince Rahotep and his wife Nofret c.2700BC.

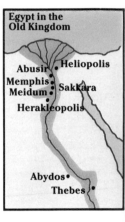

Egypt in the Old Kingdom

Abusir • Heliopolis
Memphis •
Meidum • Sakkara
Herakleopolis

Abydos •
Thebes •

Dynasty IV seems to have been torn by family feuds. Problems arose because King Khufu† had three queens. Kawab and Hetepheres II, the children of his chief queen, Meritetes, would have been the next king and queen, but Kawab died before his father. Rivalry then broke out between the sons of the two other queens. First one son ruled, then the other. The feud finally ended when the heir of one line married the heiress of the other, beginning Dynasty V.

Family tree of Dynasty IV

Sneferu = Hetepheres I

Meritetes = Khufu = Name unknown   Henutsen

Kawab = Hetepheres II = Radjedef = O

Meresankh = Khafra = O

△ Male
O Female
= Married
| Children

△   O Menkawre = O

Userkaf (1st king of Dynasty V) = O   Shepseskaf (last king of Dynasty IV)

This furniture has been reconstructed from fragments found in the tomb of Queen Hetepheres I†.

The sphinx of Gizah

Workmen building King Khufu's pyramid at Gizah were left with a large outcrop of rock. They carved it with his features and made it into the head of an enormous sphinx, a statue with a king's head and a lion's body which was a form of the sun god. The sphinx was supposed to guard the pyramids.

The cult of the sun god

The Egyptians worshipped many different gods (see page 20), but during the Old Kingdom religion was dominated by the cult of the sun god, Re, whose cult temple was at Heliopolis. The Egyptians believed that Re sailed across the sky every day in a boat. In early times people thought that when a king died he joined the northern stars. However by the time of Dynasty IV it was thought that he sailed with the sun god in his boat. 'Son of Re' became one of his most important titles.

According to a popular story, the first three kings of Dynasty V were actually the sons of Re.

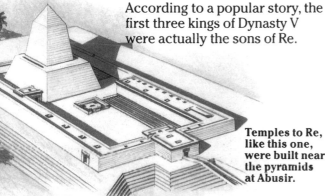

Temples to Re, like this one, were built near the pyramids at Abusir.

The Pyramid Texts

When a ruler died prayers and spells were said to enable him to join the gods in the Next World†. By the end of Dynasty V, these prayers were carved on the walls of the burial chambers of pyramids and so became known as Pyramid Texts. They were later modified and put on the sides of coffins and called Coffin Texts. By the New Kingdom, they were written on papyrus instead and placed inside the tombs. These texts are known collectively as the *Book of the Dead*.

An illustration from the *Book of the Dead*

The longest reigning king

The autobiography of Uni, a favourite courtier of Pepi I of Dynasty VI, relates how the king appointed him as a judge to try his sister-wife, Queen Imtes. After the trial, Pepi I married the two sisters of a powerful noble called Djau. Pepi's youngest son, Pepi II†, became king at a very young age and reigned for 94 years – the longest recorded reign in history.

This alabaster statue shows Pepi II with his mother, Meryre-ankhnes.

The rise of the nomarchs

In the Old Kingdom Egypt was divided into 42 *nomes* (administrative districts), each governed by an official. At first these officials did short spells of duty, and then returned to the capital of Memphis. However by Dynasty V they began to settle permanently in their *nomes* and took the title *nomarch*. They kept their positions for life and passed them on to their sons. This gradually undermined royal authority.

A *nomarch*

The First Intermediate Period

During Pepi II's reign the system was weakened by the growth of powerful officials, troubles abroad and a struggling economy. By the time he died, most of his children were already dead and so a dispute broke out over the succession. Egypt collapsed into civil conflict and confusion, and there were invasions by Libyans and bedouin† from the East. The irrigation system broke down and there was famine.

A new line of kings, Dynasties IX and X, took control in northern Egypt, ruling from Herakleopolis. However, they were unpopular in southern Egypt, especially after the Herakleopolitans sacked the holy city of Abydos. The *nomarchs* of Thebes led a revolt against them and eventually united Egypt under the Middle Kingdom (see page 26).

Key dates

c.3100BC	Egypt is united by Menes.
c.3100-2649BC	The Archaic Period
c.2649-2134BC	The Old Kingdom
c.2246-2152BC	Reign of Pepi II
c.2150-2040BC	The First Intermediate Period

Farming

The civilization of Ancient Egypt grew up along the banks of the River Nile. Egypt's wealth was based on agriculture and the river not only provided water, but also created fertile land in an area that would otherwise have been desert.

River Nile

Nile Delta

EGYPT

Ethiopian Highlands

The Nile floods

Every spring, rain and melting snow in the Highlands of Ethiopia sent a huge quantity of water down the Nile. This reached Egypt in about July. The river overflowed and flooded its banks, depositing silt (a rich, fertile mud) on the fields. This was known as the inundation. The Egyptians developed a sophisticated irrigation system to make use of the flood. However, the amount of water varied each year. Too little could result in a poor harvest and famine. Too much could damage the system and sweep away animals and entire villages.

Villages were built on high ground to avoid the floods.

Fields on higher ground, near the desert edge, were less productive as the flood did not reach them every year.

Gauges known as nilometers were built on the banks so that officials could check the water levels and plan for the year ahead.

The land was divided into small rectangular plots by a series of ditches and irrigation canals. The canals were used to store the flood water and supply it to the fields when needed. Each canal and ditch could be opened and closed.

The fields nearest to the Nile were the most fertile as the silt and water always reached them.

Farmers marked the limits of their fields with boundary stones, designed to stay in place during the floods. It was a serious crime to move the stones, or to block a neighbour's water supply.

Surveyors could be called in to redraw any boundaries damaged by the flood.

Water could be raised from a lower level to a higher one using a device called a *shaduf*. This technique is still sometimes used.

Beam

Leather bucket to carry water

Weight

What the Egyptians ate

The fertility of the land and the abundance of sources of food meant that most Egyptians had a varied diet.

Wheat and barley were used to make bread and beer, the staple elements of the Egyptian diet.

Many different vegetables were grown, including onions, leeks, garlic, beans, peas, lettuces and cucumbers.

Fruit included melons, pomegranates, grapes, dates and figs.

The farming year

The inundation season (mid-July to mid-November)

In July, when the fields were covered with flood water, work came to a halt. Some farmers could afford to relax for a while, while others were called up to work on royal building projects or mining expeditions.

The growing season (mid-November to mid-March)

As the flood subsided the farmers ploughed the land. They scattered the seeds by hand and drove animals across the fields to tread in the seeds. In the following weeks, the farmers weeded and watered the crops.

Wooden plough with bronze blade

Summer (mid-March to mid-July)

After the harvest, before the summer heat made the soil too hard to dig, the irrigation channels had to be repaired and new ones dug, ready for the next flood. This was done as part of the labour tax everybody paid to the king.

The harvest (March to April)

The harvest was in March and April. Before it was gathered taxmen came to assess how much grain each field would yield. From that they calculated how much each farmer should give to the king in taxes.

Men cut off the ears of grain, using sickles with flint blades. The stalks were later gathered and used for animal food.

Flint sickle

Some farmers had flute players to provide music while people worked.

Women and children picked up any ears of grain which the men had missed.

Cattle were driven over the ears to separate the grain from the stalk. This is known as threshing.

The grain was stored in granaries.

The ears of grain were taken to the threshing-floor.

Drinking water was kept under a tree or in a shelter to keep it cool.

Threshing-floor

Women separated the grain from the husk by winnowing (tossing it in the air so that the light husks blew away).

Honey from bees kept in pottery hives (shown above) was used as a sweetener. Oil for cooking was made from linseed, saffron and sesame.

Several breeds of cattle and pigs were kept.

Sheep and goats provided dairy produce and hides.

Egyptians kept geese, ducks and pigeons and caught many varieties of wildfowl.

Fish were caught in traps, by hook and line, and in nets hung between two boats. Large fish were speared.

15

Pyramids and tombs

In an attempt to preserve their bodies forever, the Egyptian kings had massive tombs built for themselves and their families. Pyramid-shaped tombs were introduced during the Old Kingdom.

However pyramids were frequently robbed, so the New Kingdom kings chose to be buried in tombs cut deep into the sides of cliffs. For more about how pyramids were built, see page 52

Mastabas

The first kings were buried under mud-brick buildings called *mastabas*. This is a reconstruction of one built at Sakkara in about 3100BC.

Step pyramids

At the beginning of Dynasty III, King Zoser's† architect, Imhotep†, designed a new style of tomb. He built a stone *mastaba*, enlarged it, then added other layers on top, each smaller than the last. This resulted in the first step pyramid. Experts

believe that the steps were intended as a symbolic staircase up which the king climbed to reach the stars. Step pyamids were planned by all the later kings of Dynasty III, but only Zoser's and Huni's (see opposite) were completed.

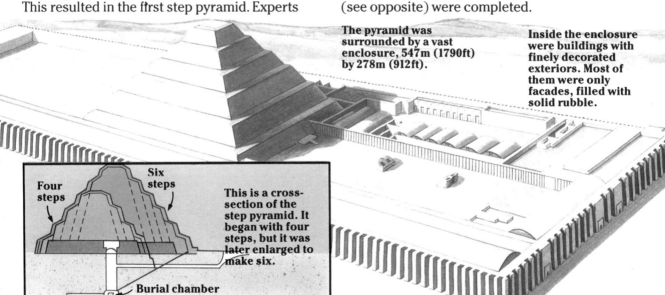

The pyramid was surrounded by a vast enclosure, 547m (1790ft) by 278m (912ft).

Inside the enclosure were buildings with finely decorated exteriors. Most of them were only facades, filled with solid rubble.

Four steps

Six steps

This is a cross-section of the step pyramid. It began with four steps, but it was later enlarged to make six.

Burial chamber

Private tombs

Ordinary Egyptians were simply buried in a hole in the sand and covered with a layer of sand and stones. Those who could afford it had a deep shaft cut, with one or more chambers at the bottom.

The tombs of the wealthiest people were decorated inside with scenes of daily life. The Egyptians believed this ensured that these activities carried on after death.

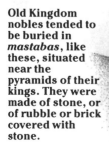

Old Kingdom nobles tended to be buried in *mastabas*, like these, situated near the pyramids of their kings. They were made of stone, or of rubble or brick covered with stone.

This painting is from a noble's tomb in the cliffs at Beni Hasan. Cliff-cut tombs were in use from the end of the Old Kingdom.

These tombs were built by the royal tomb builders at Deir el Medinah (see page 66) for themselves.

Straight-sided pyramids

The introduction of the worship of the sun god, Re (see page 13), at the end of Dynasty III affected the design of pyramids. The steps were replaced by straight sides. These represented a solid form of the sun's rays, up which the king could climb to reach his 'father' Re.

All the early pyramids were made of stone, but most kings in Dynasty XII used mud-brick, which did not wear as well. There was an outer casing of limestone, but this was often stolen, leaving the bricks exposed.

This reconstruction is based on the pyramid of King Sahure at Abusir.

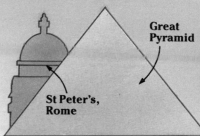

Enclosure wall

Smaller pyramid for the queen

Daily offerings were made to the spirit of the king in the mortuary temple.

Huni's pyramid at Meidum

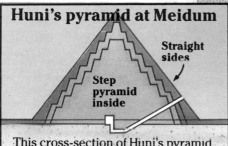

Straight sides

Step pyramid inside

This cross-section of Huni's pyramid shows the transition between the styles. It began as a step pyramid, but Huni's son, Sneferu†, added straight sides.

A covered causeway linked the valley and mortuary temples.

The king's body may have been prepared for burial on the roof of the valley temple, which was on the edge of the Nile.

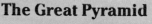

The Great Pyramid

Great Pyramid

St Peter's, Rome

The Great Pyramid at Gizah was built for King Cheops (or Khufu†) of Dynasty IV. It was known as one of the Seven Wonders of the Ancient World because of its size – 146m (480ft) high. This shows its height compared with St Peter's in Rome, the biggest cathedral in the world.

Mentuhotep's temple

King Mentuhotep II† of Dynasty XI built himself a unique monument on the West Bank of the Nile at Thebes, combining a funerary temple and tomb. His successors planned similar monuments, but never completed them.

Some experts believe there may have been a small pyramid on top.

The Valley of the Kings

The New Kingdom kings and their families were buried in tombs cut into cliffs, situated in two remote valleys (the Valley of the Kings and the Valley of the Queens) on the West Bank of the Nile opposite Thebes. Although the tombs were inconspicuous from the outside, the insides were lavishly decorated.

Death and burial

The Egyptians saw death as a transitional stage in the progress to a better life in the Next World†. They believed they could only reach their full potential after death. Each person was thought to have three souls – the *ka*, the *ba* and the *akh*. For these to function properly, it was considered essential for the body to survive intact. The Egyptians tried various methods to achieve this. In predynastic Upper Egypt, bodies were buried in shallow graves. They dried out quickly in the hot sand and so were largely preserved from decay.

A preserved body from an early grave, c.3200BC.

Embalming

During the Archaic Period, kings and nobles were buried deep under the ground in stone-lined burial chambers. Away from contact with the hot sand, the bodies decayed. So the Egyptians tried to find artificial ways to preserve them instead. By the New Kingdom an elaborate process of embalming had evolved, which was used by kings, nobles and those who could afford it.

When the person died, priests recited prayers and a final attempt was made to revive the corpse. It was then washed and purified in a special shelter called an *ibu*.

The body was then taken to the *wabet*, the embalmers' workshop. First a cut was made in the left side. The organs were removed and stored in containers known as canopic jars.

Canopic jars

A salt called natron was packed around the body to dry it out. After a few days, the insides were filled with linen or sawdust, resin and natron. The body was wrapped in bandages, with jewellery and amulets† (shown here) between the layers.

A portrait mask was placed over the head by the chief embalmer, who wore a jackal mask to represent Anubis*, the patron god of embalmers. The wrapped body, or mummy, was put in a coffin.

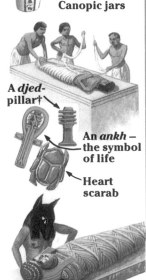

A *djed-pillar*†

An *ankh* – the symbol of life

Heart scarab

Coffins

Early coffins were wooden and rectangular. In the Old Kingdom they were plain or decorated with a band of *hieroglyphs*. Middle Kingdom coffins, like this one, were more ornate.

Coffins were often elaborately decorated with spells.

These eyes, called *udjat* † eyes, were meant to protect the mummy.

Anthropoid (human-shaped) coffins came into use during the Middle Kingdom and remained in fashion for over 2000 years. By the New Kingdom, mummies were placed inside a nest of two or three coffins.

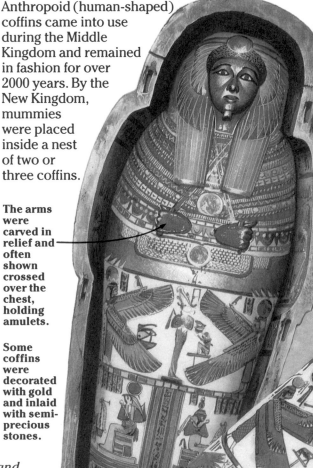

The arms were carved in relief and often shown crossed over the chest, holding amulets.

Some coffins were decorated with gold and inlaid with semi-precious stones.

18 *For more about Anubis and other Egyptian gods and goddesses, see pages 20-21.*

The funeral

The body was taken to the tomb in a procession of family and friends. The funeral of a nobleman or woman also included professional mourners, priests, animals for sacrifice and porters carrying the dead person's belongings.

At the tomb door the priest performed the 'Opening of the Mouth' ceremony. This was supposed to revive the dead person's bodily functions and powers. Final prayers were said.

The wooden coffin was placed inside a *sarcophagus* (stone coffin), and the lid was closed. The burial chamber was sealed, although the upper chambers of the tomb were left open so that regular offerings of food could be left.

The Next World

The Egyptians believed in a life after death, which they referred to as the Next World. Although they had several different versions of what it would be like, it was thought to be a happy land somewhere in the far west. (It was often called the Kingdom of the West.) Entry depended on leading a virtuous life on Earth. When a person died he or she first had to go through a series of tests and ordeals.

First the dead man had to persuade an old ferryman to take him across the River of Death.

Then he had to pass through the Twelve Gates, guarded by serpents. The dead man had amulets and a *Book of the Dead*, containing spells, a map and information to help him by-pass the many dangers.

After passing by the Lake of Fire, he had to confront the 42 Assessors who read out a list of sins. The dead man had to swear that he had never committed any of them.

If he passed this test, he entered the Judgement Hall of Osiris, where his heart was weighed against the Feather of Truth. If he had led a sinful life his heart would be heavy. The scales would tip against him and he would be fed to a monster. If he had led a virtuous life his heart would balance with the Feather of Truth. The man could then join his ancestors in the Kingdom of the West. This papyrus showing the 'Weighing of the Heart' is from the *Book of the Dead* (see page 13).

Egyptian gods and goddesses

The Egyptians had as many as 2000 gods and goddesses. Some, such as Amun, were worshipped throughout the whole country, while others had only a local following. The most important gods had a home town where their main temple, known as a cult temple, was situated. They were also worshipped at other shrines and temples across the country. A few deities, such as Bes and Tawaret, had no temples, but were worshipped in people's homes. Some gods and goddesses represented forces of nature, such as water or air. Others were associated with aspects of daily life, such as weaving or farming. From predynastic times, many deities were identified with particular animals or birds (and sometimes with plants too). To make them easier to recognize, they were often shown in paintings and carvings with the head of that creature. Many of the gods and goddesses were linked in families. Here are some of the most important ones.

◄ There were many different versions of the sun god, or creator, but the most common was **Re**.

Re

Shu*, son of Re, was god of air.

Nut

Shu

Geb

Shu's daughter, **Nut**, was the sky goddess. She was married to her brother, **Geb**, god of the Earth.

◄ **Amun**, was King of the Gods in the New Kingdom. He was associated with Re and became known as **Amun-Re**. Temple: Karnak. Animals: goose and ram.

Amun

Mut

Mut, wife of Amun, was a mother goddess. Temple: Karnak. Animal: lioness.

Khonsu

Khonsu, son of Amun and Mut, was the moon god. ► Temple: Karnak.

Ptah was patron of Memphis. Animal: Apis bull†. ▼

Sekhmet, wife of Ptah, represented motherhood and the destructive power of the sun. Animal: lioness. ▼

◄ **Osiris**, the son and heir of Geb and Nut was King of Egypt and introduced vines and grain. He became Ruler of the Dead. Temple: Abydos. His sister-wife, **Isis**, introduced crafts. Temple: Philae.

Horus

Hathor

Ptah —— **Sekhmet**

Nefertem, son of Ptah and Sekhmet, was god of oils ► and perfumes. Flower: sacred blue lotus.

Nefertem

Set —— **Nepthys** —— **Osiris** —— **Isis**

▲ **Set**, was god of deserts, storms and trouble. Animals: ass, pig and hippopotamus. He was married to his sister **Nepthys**.

Anubis, son of Osiris and Nepthys, was god of the dead and embalming. Animal: jackal. ▼

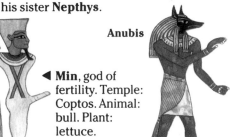

Anubis

Min

◄ **Min**, god of fertility. Temple: Coptos. Animal: bull. Plant: lettuce.

Horus, inherited the throne of Egypt. Temple: Edfu. Animal: falcon.

Ihy, son of Horus and Hathor, was the musician god.

Hathor, wife of Horus, was goddess of love, beauty and joy. A mother and death goddess. Temple: Denderah. Animal: cow.

Neith

◄ **Neith** was mother of the sun, goddess of hunting, war and weaving, and guardian of the Red Crown of Lower Egypt. Temple: Sais. Symbol: shield and arrows.

Shu, as god of air, is often shown holding up Nut, the sky goddess.

Sobek

◄ **Sobek** was god of water. He was married to Renenutet. Temples: Fayum and Kom Ombo. Animal: Crocodile.

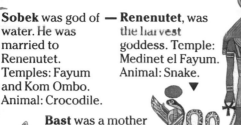

Thoth

— **Renenutet**, was the harvest goddess. Temple: Medinet el Fayum. Animal: Snake.

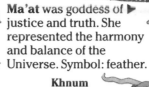

Ma'at was goddess of ▶ justice and truth. She represented the harmony and balance of the Universe. Symbol: feather.

Ma'at

Satis

Khnum

Anukis

Bast

Bast was a mother goddess who represented the healing power of the sun. Temple: Bubastis. Animal: cat. Her son was **Mithos**, the lion-headed god.

Renenutet

Thoth was god of wisdom and vizier and scribe of the gods. Temple: Hermopolis. Animal: baboon. Bird: ibis.

Bes the dwarf ▶ was the jester of the gods. He protected people's homes and children.

Bes

Taweret, a ▶ female hippopotamus, looked after pregnant women and babies.

Taweret

Khnum was a ▶ potter who created people on his potter's wheel. He was thought to control the source of the Nile. Temple: Elephantine. Animal: ram.

Khnum's wife, **Satis**, was patroness of hunters.

Their daughter, **Anukis**, was ▲ goddess of the First Cataract† of the River Nile.

The creation

The Egyptians had many tales about how the world began. According to one legend, it started with an ocean in darkness. Then a mound of dry land rose up and the sun god Re appeared. He created light and all things. Here are four other different versions of the story.

The sun god flew to an island as a falcon.

He emerged from a sacred blue lotus that grew out of the mud.

He was hatched from an egg laid by a goose called the Great Cackler.

He appeared as a scarab beetle on the eastern horizon.

The story of Osiris and Set

The Egyptians believed that Osiris and Isis had once ruled Egypt. They were good and much-loved rulers, but their brother Set was jealous. He invited Osiris to a party where he produced a beautiful casket, and announced he would give it to the person who fitted most exactly inside. The casket had secretly been made for Osiris, and once he was inside, Set had it tossed into the Nile. The current carried it into the Mediterranean, and on to Byblos. There it was cast ashore and a huge tree grew around it.

After many adventures, Isis found the body and returned with it to Egypt. Despite her attempts to hide it, Set discovered the body and cut it into pieces. However Isis and her stepson Anubis reassembled them and succeeded in bringing Osiris back to life. In revenge Set tried to harm Horus, the son and heir of Osiris and Isis. He took Horus to court, claiming he had no right to rule, and a series of battles followed. Horus finally won. He became King of Egypt, while Osiris ruled the Kingdom of the Dead.

Early civilization in India

Little is known about the emergence of early civilization in India, but it seems to have developed from small communities which were established in the Indus Valley by about 3000BC. The people made their living chiefly from farming, and later from trade. The produce and artefacts of farmers and craftsmen paid for imports from abroad, including precious metals and cloth.

The remains of over a hundred towns have been found. The most impressive ruins are those of the cities of Mohenjo Daro and Harappa, which seem to have controlled the entire area. Information from excavations there has been used in this reconstruction of Mohenjo Daro.

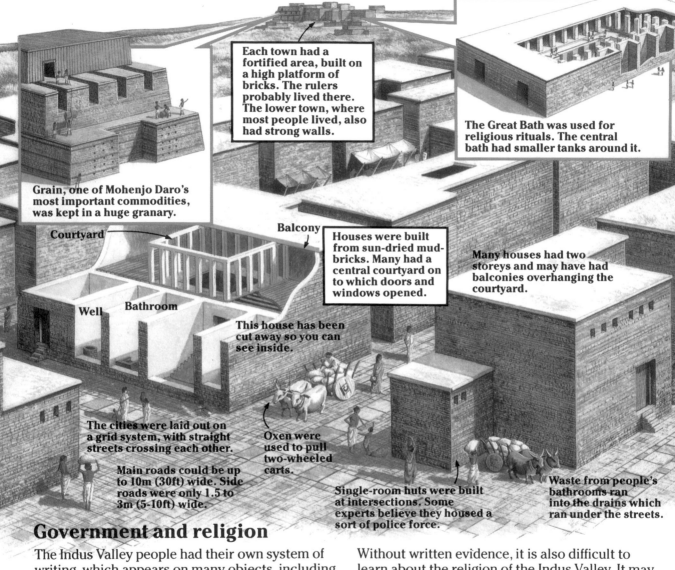

Each town had a fortified area, built on a high platform of bricks. The rulers probably lived there. The lower town, where most people lived, also had strong walls.

The Great Bath was used for religious rituals. The central bath had smaller tanks around it.

Grain, one of Mohenjo Daro's most important commodities, was kept in a huge granary.

Courtyard

Balcony

Houses were built from sun-dried mud-bricks. Many had a central courtyard on to which doors and windows opened.

Many houses had two storeys and may have had balconies overhanging the courtyard.

Well   Bathroom

This house has been cut away so you can see inside.

The cities were laid out on a grid system, with straight streets crossing each other.

Main roads could be up to 10m (30ft) wide. Side roads were only 1.5 to 3m (5-10ft) wide.

Oxen were used to pull two-wheeled carts.

Single-room huts were built at intersections. Some experts believe they housed a sort of police force.

Waste from people's bathrooms ran into the drains which ran under the streets.

Government and religion

The Indus Valley people had their own system of writing, which appears on many objects, including carved seals. No-one has yet been able to interpret it, so we know little about their system of government. The cities may have been ruled by kings, but no royal tombs have been discovered.

Without written evidence, it is also difficult to learn about the religion of the Indus Valley. It may be that the political leaders were priests as well. There are no buildings that can be identified as temples, so people may have worshipped in their homes. Some information comes from artefacts.

◀ This seated male figure, surrounded by animals, may be a very early version of the Hindu god Siva.

◀ Baked clay figures like this one suggest that goddesses played a leading role.

This statue may ▶ be of an Indus Valley ruler or priest.

◀ Carved seals

The civilization declines

Gradually, from about 1800BC, the Indus Valley civilization declined. The reasons for this are unclear, but there seems to have been frequent flooding, and the inhabitants overgrazed the land and cut down the trees. Excavations show a decline in trade and in the quality of the buildings. Finally war may have destroyed at least some centres, including Mohenjo Daro.

The date of the final collapse is uncertain, but it may have been connected with the arrival in about 1500BC of groups of Indo-Europeans† who called themselves Aryas (known in the West as Aryans). They occupied the Indus Valley and then drifted eastwards into the Ganges Valley.

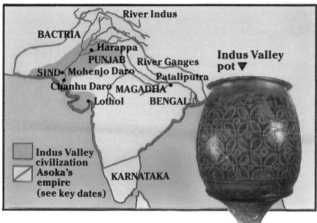

The Aryans

Much of our information about the Aryans comes from an ancient series of religious poems composed by priests. The poems were passed on by word of mouth, and by 900BC they were gathered together to form a collection called the *Rig Veda* (Later three other *vedas* were composed.) The *Rig Veda* describes the events of the period. The Aryans set up several kingdoms, each with its own *rajah* (ruler). Most people were farmers and wealth was counted in terms of the number of cattle a man owned. In their leisure hours they enjoyed music, dancing and gambling.

During this period, class divisions started to assume an important role. There was a class for priests, another for warriors, and one for farmers and traders. At the bottom came the Dravidians (the original inhabitants), and the children of mixed Aryan-Dravidian marriages. This formed the basis for the caste† system, which has lasted into the 20th century.

By the 6th century BC some important changes had taken place. The centre of Aryan power had moved to the Ganges Basin, where four rulers struggled to gain control of the whole area. The Aryans had adopted an irrigation system and were growing new crops and using domesticated elephants. Skilled craftsmen had emerged, and specialist traders, such as merchants, moneylenders and entertainers. Money and a new writing system were both in use.

Religion

The Aryans worshipped several deities, particularly those connected with the sky. These included Indra (god of war and weather), Varuna (who governed the order of the Universe) and Mitra (protector of oaths and contracts). Sacrifices† played an important part in their worship and, as rituals grew more complex, the training and status of priests increased.

The Aryans believed that after death a person's soul passed into a new body and that behaviour in one life affected the quality of the next. Holy men gave up their possessions and wandered around preaching, trying to achieve an inner joy through poverty and meditation. These ideas, and others, provided the basis for a new religion, Buddhism, founded by Gautama, an Indian prince. He became the Buddha, 'the Enlightened One', and his teachings spread rapidly across the Far East.

Head of the Buddha from Gandhara

Key dates

c.3000BC Farming communities are established in northwest India.

c.2500BC The Indus Valley civilization reaches its peak.

c.1800BC Signs of decline appear in some Indus Valley sites

c.1500BC Arrival of the Aryans

c.560-483BC Life of the Buddha

512BC King Darius† of Persia conquers the provinces of Gandhara and Sind.

327-325BC Alexander the Great† of Macedonia campaigns in India.

c.321BC Chandragupta founds the Maurya Dynasty (c.321-185BC).

305BC An invasion by Seleucus Nicator, ruler of the Seleucid† empire, is defeated by Chandragupta.

c.272-231BC Asoka, grandson of Chandragupta, unites most of India under his rule (see map) and is converted to Buddhism. His empire is divided after his death and the Mauryas decline in power.

c.185BC The Sunga Dynasty replaces the Mauryas. Greeks from Bactria (formerly part of the Seleucid empire) invade and set up small kingdoms in the Punjab.

After Sumer

By about 2500BC the area which stretched from the northern borders of Sumer (see pages 6-8) to the eastern borders of Egypt was inhabited by people known as Semites. The Semites spoke closely related dialects which form part of the language group known by modern scholars as Semitic. Sumerian culture had a strong influence on the region and many of the neighbouring Semitic tribes wanted to share in its wealth.

Akkad

The Akkadians, a Semitic people from a land just north of Sumer, adopted Sumerian culture, religion and writing from the earliest times. In 2371BC*, an Akkadian called Sargon seized the throne of the Sumerian city of Kish. He was a gifted soldier and administrator and created the first great Mesopotamian empire.

Sargon conquered the whole of Akkad and Sumer, uniting them under his rule, and so the city states† lost their independence. He also took control of Elam, a land east of the Tigris, and set up a vassal† as governor. He marched as far as the Mediterranean, conquering cities such as Mari and Ebla (see opposite) on the way. Sargon's empire fell apart after his death, but it was reconquered by his grandson, Naram-Sin†(2291-2255BC).

Sargon of Akkad

Trouble broke out again in about 2230BC, and the kingdom finally collapsed after local rebellions and invasions by tribes of Gutians from the Zagros mountains.

Northern Mesopotamia

In northern Mesopotamia there were independent cities strongly influenced by Sumerian culture. The greatest of these was Mari, which was an important trading post, both for river traffic and for overland caravans (expeditions crossing the desert).

Statue of Itur-Shamagan, King of Mari

The nomads

To the south and east of the Fertile Crescent lived groups of nomadic† Semitic tribes who wandered the edges of the deserts seeking pasture for their sheep, goats and donkeys. They came to towns and villages to trade animals, wool and artefacts for grain, dates and metal goods. Some worked as mercenaries† or labourers and a few managed to acquire land and become farmers. Others took to raiding villages and caravans. The nomads were usually easily absorbed into village life, but their numbers sometimes increased to such an extent that they threatened the stability of the city states.

Semitic nomads from a painting at Beni Hasan, Egypt

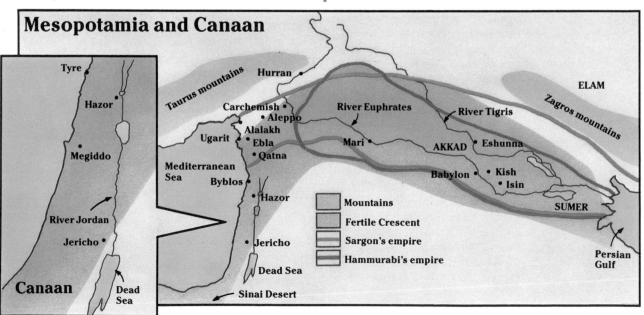

Mesopotamia and Canaan

Tyre
Hazor
Megiddo
River Jordan
Jericho
Canaan
Dead Sea

Taurus mountains
Hurran
Carchemish
Aleppo
Alalakh
Ugarit
Ebla
Qatna
Mediterranean Sea
Byblos
Hazor
Jericho
Dead Sea
Sinai Desert

River Euphrates
Mari
River Tigris
AKKAD
Eshunna
Babylon
Kish
Isin
SUMER
ELAM
Zagros mountains
Persian Gulf

Mountains
Fertile Crescent
Sargon's empire
Hammurabi's empire

Canaan

The area known as Canaan stretched from the borders of the Sinai Desert north into what is now southern Syria. By the Early Bronze Age (c.3000-2000BC), it was divided into independent city states, each with massive fortifications, palaces and temples. In the farmland around the cities, animals were raised and barley, wheat, grapes, olives and vegetables were grown. The northern cities on the east-west trade route were among the largest. One of the most impressive was Ebla, which is reconstructed here.

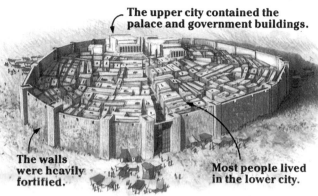

The upper city contained the palace and government buildings.

The walls were heavily fortified.

Most people lived in the lower city.

The ports of Canaan, such as Byblos, and the north Syrian port of Ugarit, were great trading centres. They exported cedarwood, metals, ivory and textiles (including a rare purple-dyed cloth) throughout the eastern Mediterranean. Egyptian influence was strong, especially in Byblos, but merchants also came from Cyprus, Mesopotamia and Anatolia. In about 2350BC southern Canaan

went into decline. Some cities were abandoned, others were destroyed. It is uncertain what caused this as there were no written records, but it may have been due to local political upheavals.

Enamelled pendant from Byblos, showing Egyptian influence

At the beginning of the Middle Bronze Age (c.2000-1500BC), a new period of prosperity began. The Canaanites invented their own form of writing, a simple alphabetic script of 27 picture signs. It was used for short inscriptions only. All dealings between foreigners were conducted in Akkadian, which was written in *cuneiform* (see page 10). The Canaanite city states were well-situated for trade. In the Late Bronze Age (c.1550-1150BC) the Egyptians, Mitannians* and Hittites* fought over them and divided them between themselves.

Canaanite religion

The Canaanites had many gods and goddesses, who they worshipped in temples and in 'high places' – hill-top enclosures containing large upright stone structures.

Baal was god of rain, storms, fertility and war. His cult† animal was a bull.

The Amorites

One group of nomadic Semites, the Amorites, threatened both Mesopotamia and Canaan in about 2000BC. They conquered Sumer, Akkad and Assyria and set up dynasties in the city states of Canaan. These dynasties fought each other for supremacy, but were soon overshadowed by the rise of the Assyrians (see pages 74-75).

In 1792BC a young man called Hammurabi† inherited the throne of Babylon, a small Amorite kingdom in central Mesopotamia. The kingdom had been founded about a hundred years earlier, but Hammurabi extended its frontiers to include all of Sumer and Akkad. He also defeated the Gutians and took over territory from the Elamites and the Assyrians. Hammurabi was a clever administrator and diplomat, and was concerned with law, order and the welfare of his people.

Hammurabi established a unified system of laws and penalties within his expanding kingdom. This stone *stela*† records his code of laws.

Hammurabi's empire slowly declined after his death and in about 1595BC the ruler of Babylon was overthrown by Hittites who plundered the city. This left the way open for new rulers – the Kassites*.

Key dates

c.3000-2000BC Independent city states flourish in Sumer, Akkad and Canaan.

c.2371-2316BC Reign of Sargon of Akkad

c.2300BC Southern Canaan is in decline.

c.2291-2255BC Reign of Naram-Sin of Akkad

c.2230BC Akkad collapses after invasions by Gutians.

c.2000BC Increasing numbers of Amorites move into Canaan and Mesopotamia.

c.2000-1550BC New period of prosperity in Canaan

c.1894BC Amorites establish a dynasty in the city of Babylon.

c.1792-1750BC Reign of Hammurabi of Babylon

c.1595BC Hittites plunder Babylon and depose the ruler.

c.1550-1150BC Canaanite city states are divided between Egyptians, Mitannians and Hittites.

For more about the Mitannians, the Hittites and the Kassites, see pages 44-45.

The Middle Kingdom (c.2040-1640BC)

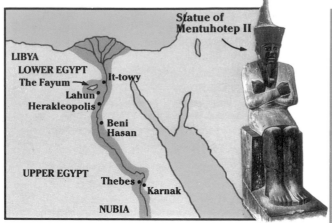

Statue of Mentuhotep II

LIBYA
LOWER EGYPT
The Fayum
Lahun
Herakleopolis
It-towy
Beni Hasan
UPPER EGYPT
Thebes
Karnak
NUBIA

In about 2040BC, the ruler of Thebes, Mentuhotep II†, defeated the Herakleopolitan king (see page 13) and reunited Egypt under Dynasty XI. This began the period known as the Middle Kingdom. Mentuhotep drove invaders from the Delta and crushed all opposition to his rule, appointing loyal Thebans to key posts in the government. From his capital at Thebes, he resumed foreign trading contacts and embarked on an energetic programme to restore Egyptian prosperity.

The soldiers' tomb

Archaeologists have excavated a tomb next to Mentuhotep's funeral monument (see page 17), which contains the bodies of about 60 soldiers, many of whom were archers. No-one knows why they were buried near a place normally reserved for the royal family. Their bodies had many wounds, so they may have been the Thebans who died in the battle that brought Mentuhotep to power.

Tomb models

In the First Intermediate Period it had become the custom to put wooden models in graves, showing scenes from everyday life, such as making bread and beer. Meket-re†, Mentuhotep III's chancellor, had a huge model collection in his tomb. It included models of a house and garden, and several boats.

Tomb models showing men catching fish

Noblemen's barges

Dynasty XII

A rebellion during the reign of Mentuhotep IV led to the emergence of a new dynasty in about 1991BC. The new king, who had been an important official in Dynasty XI, called himself Amenemhat I†, meaning 'Amun is foremost'. Amun* became the patron god of the royal family and grew in importance. A festival was introduced in his honour, called the Feast of the Valley.

During the Feast of the Valley, Amun's statue was taken in its sacred boat from the temple at Karnak across the Nile to the necropolis† on the West Bank.

Amenemhat's dynasty became one of the most successful to rule Egypt, presiding over a period of power, wealth and artistic achievement. However Amenemhat was conscious of the weakness of his claim to the throne and of the need to secure the succession. In the twentieth year of his reign, he had his son Senusret I crowned as a co-king. Amenemhat was murdered ten years later, but Senusret succeeded in holding on to power.

Very few Middle Kingdom buildings have survived. This chapel built by Senusret I was later dismantled but has been reconstructed by archaeologists.

Throughout Dynasty XII Egypt's frontiers were secure. Libyans who had settled in the rich farmland of the Western Delta during the First Intermediate Period were driven out. The Libyans were one of the most important of the 'Nine Bows', Egypt's traditional enemies. On the eastern frontier, a string of great forts was built. The garrisons there kept a check on the bedouin†, although they allowed them in temporarily to trade and pasture their flocks in the Delta. The Egyptians occupied Nubia (see page 28) and fortresses were built to guard the new frontier there.

A Libyan soldier

For more about Amun and other Egyptian gods and goddesses, see pages 20-21.

A new capital

In order to keep better control of the 'Two Lands', Amenemhat moved the capital north to It-towy, near the Fayum (a huge dip in the desert to the west of the Nile Valley). The Fayum had once contained a vast lake that was filled from the Nile, but silt had built up round the entrance, forming a fertile tongue of land.

Senusret II began to reclaim more land by reducing the amount of water flowing into the lake. New land became available for farming and many building projects were undertaken. A royal palace was built at Kahun, as well as a town for the priests and officials who looked after Senusret's pyramid at nearby Lahun.

Art and culture

Egyptian art and culture flourished under Dynasty XII. In particular many fine statues were produced.

◀ Most earlier Egyptian scupltures were idealized portraits, like this one of a noblewoman called Sennul.

Some Middle Kingdom artists produced more individual portraits, like this face of Senusret III. ▼

▲ From Dynasty XII, some statues were cube-shaped and showed the person squatting.

The cult of Osiris

The cult of Osiris, ruler of the dead, grew in popularity during the Middle Kingdom. Evidence of this is shown by inscriptions and objects found in tombs. In earlier times Egyptians had expected the king to look after their interests after death. But in the chaos of the First Intermediate Period (see page 13), many people lost their faith in kings and turned instead to Osiris. He promised a happy life after death as a reward for a good and virtuous life on earth.

The nomarchs

At the beginning of the Middle Kingdom, the provincial governors, or *nomarchs*, still played a part in local government, ruling from their palaces in the provincial capitals. However, under Senusret III† a reorganization of government took place and the role of the *nomarchs* declined. The Vizier, the king's chief minister, was given control of the government departments and Egypt was divided into three administrative areas, each called a *waret*.

The paintings in the tombs of the *nomarchs* provide a detailed picture of the daily life of the period. This painting, of men and baboons picking figs, is from Beni Hasan.

Dynasties XIII and XIV

When the direct male line died out, a princess called Sobek-neferu† became the last 'king' of Dynasty XII. The whole system of centralized government based on a king and a strong succession broke down. The kings of Dynasty XIII were often unrelated to one another and ruled for very short periods. For the next hundred years real power was in the hands of important families of officials. Government became less and less efficient. Eventually some princes from the Western Delta broke away and formed Dynasty XIV, ruling at the same time as Dynasty XIII.

The forts were no longer properly maintained and the Egyptians lost control of Nubia. People from the Middle East who had settled in Egypt began to take over towns in the Eastern Delta. In 1674BC, the Delta was overrun by a group known as Hyksos†, who later became the rulers of Dynasties XV and XVI. This marked the beginning of a period of decline, known as the Second Intermediate Period (see page 45).

The king began wearing a blue crown called the *khepresh*.

(see page 45)

Key dates

c.2040BC Mentuhotep II reunites Egypt under Dynasty XI. The Middle Kingdom begins.

c.1991-1783BC Dynasty XII

c.1783-1640BC Dynasty XIII

c.1674BC The Eastern Delta is overrun with people from the Middle East.

c.1640-1552BC The Second Intermediate Period

Nubia

Nubia was the land that lay immediately south of Egypt. It was hotter and less fertile than Egypt, but there was enough vegetation in the Nile Valley and at oases to support herds of cattle. These played an important part in the Nubian way of life.

The earliest cultures of Egypt and Nubia were very similar, but from about 3300BC Egypt began developing much more quickly. From Dynasty I, Egyptian kings sent expeditions to Nubia in search of valuable raw materials, such as gold, copper, cattle, slaves and semi-precious stones. Beyond Nubia they found exotic animals, such as giraffes and monkeys, and such rare items as ivory, incense, panther skins, ostrich eggs and plumes, and ebony (a hard black wood).

This painting shows Nubians offering gifts.

Nubia during the Old Kingdom

The aim of Egyptian foreign policy was to keep the country's frontiers secure and to protect trading interests. In Dynasty IV, King Sneferu† launched a devastating attack on Nubia. Egyptian records claim that 70,000 prisoners were taken. Excavations confirm that there was a sharp drop in Nubia's population and wealth.

The Egyptians built a heavily fortified town at Buhen as a base from which to trade with Nubia and the African interior. At first trade was under the direct control of the king, but later some of his powers were delegated to *nomarchs* (see page 13). The *nomarch* of Aswan was given the title 'Keeper of the Gate of the South'.

The Nubian recovery

By the time of Egyptian Dynasty VI, the Nubians were showing signs of recovery. They became involved in clashes with desert nomads†, making trade routes dangerous for the Egyptians. During the First Intermediate Period the Egyptians lost their position of power and Nubia came under the control of native Nubian princes. Archaeologists describe the Nubians of this time as 'C-group'.

Nubia during the Middle Kingdom

Trading contacts between Egypt and Nubia were resumed during the Middle Kingdom. The Egyptians soon felt threatened by the presence of prosperous, independent Nubians in the Nile Valley and so they invaded Nubia again. By the end of the reign of Senusret I, Nubia had been conquered up to the Second Cataract†.

Also seen as a threat was the Kingdom of Kush, situated in the area around the Third Cataract. In order to protect their new frontier, the Egyptians built a string of nine fortresses around the Second Cataract. These fortresses were masterpieces of military engineering and design, as well as centres of trade and government. The reconstruction shown here is based on ruins at Buhen.

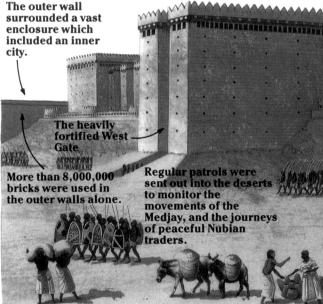

The outer wall surrounded a vast enclosure which included an inner city.

The heavily fortified West Gate

More than 8,000,000 bricks were used in the outer walls alone.

Regular patrols were sent out into the deserts to monitor the movements of the Medjay, and the journeys of peaceful Nubian traders.

The Second Intermediate Period in Nubia

After Dynasty XIII, the Egyptians lost control of Nubia. Traces of a terrible fire at Buhen and evidence of Kushite pottery there suggest that the Kushites took over. Egyptian sources describe independent kings in Nubia who formed alliances with the Hyksos†. Some of the Medjay† were hostile to the Kushites and joined the armies of the Egyptian kings who ruled from Thebes (see page 45).

Kushite pottery

The Buhen horse

The first known example of a horse in Egypt was found in an excavation of a Middle Kingdom site at Buhen. Horses had only just been introduced in the Middle East at this time, and did not become common in Egypt until much later. An official might have brought it back from the East and taken it with him to Nubia.

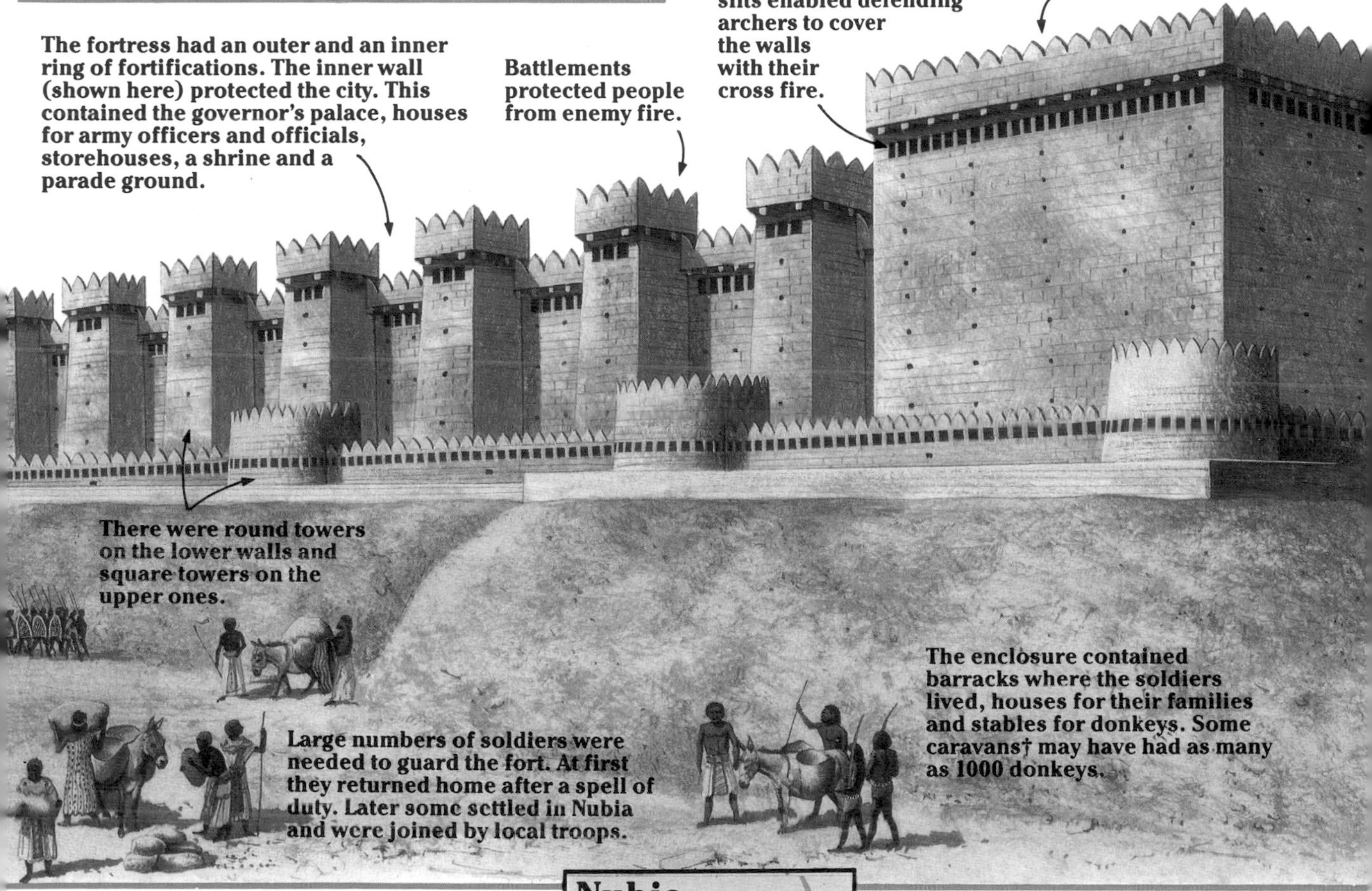

There was a secret tunnel to the Nile, so water and supplies could be brought in during a siege. Stone quays on the river enabled ships to dock.

The upper walls were 11m (36ft) high and 4.5m (14ft) thick. Objects could be dropped on the heads of attackers from an overhang at the top.

The fortress had an outer and an inner ring of fortifications. The inner wall (shown here) protected the city. This contained the governor's palace, houses for army officers and officials, storehouses, a shrine and a parade ground.

Battlements protected people from enemy fire.

Carefully positioned arrow slits enabled defending archers to cover the walls with their cross fire.

There were round towers on the lower walls and square towers on the upper ones.

Large numbers of soldiers were needed to guard the fort. At first they returned home after a spell of duty. Later some settled in Nubia and were joined by local troops.

The enclosure contained barracks where the soldiers lived, houses for their families and stables for donkeys. Some caravans† may have had as many as 1000 donkeys.

Nubia in the New Kingdom

The temple of Abu Simbel was one of seven temples built in Nubia by Ramesses II.

The Egyptians invaded Nubia again during the New Kingdom and extended their frontier to the Fourth Cataract. A viceroy† known as the 'King's Son of Kush' was appointed to rule Nubia. Nubians adopted Egyptian culture and religion and became loyal subjects.

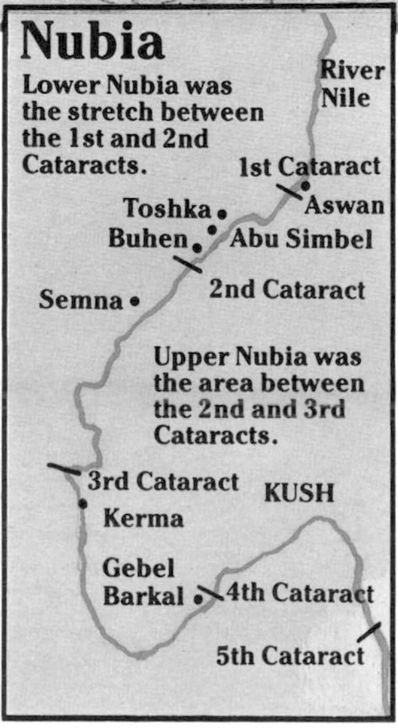

Nubia

Lower Nubia was the stretch between the 1st and 2nd Cataracts.

Upper Nubia was the area between the 2nd and 3rd Cataracts.

River Nile

1st Cataract
Aswan
Toshka
Buhen • Abu Simbel
Semna •
2nd Cataract

3rd Cataract   KUSH
Kerma
Gebel Barkal • 4th Cataract
5th Cataract

Key dates

c.2900BC Nubians of this period are known as 'A-group'. Egyptian kings begin campaigning in Nubia.

c.2570BC King Sneferu of Egypt attacks Nubia.

c.2300BC Nubians recovery; Nubians at this time are known as 'C-group'.

c.2200BC Egypt loses control of Nubia.

By **1926BC** Egypt reconquers Nubia up to the 2nd Cataract and builds fortresses.

c.1600BC Egypt loses control of Nubia again and Kushites take over.

c.1550-1300BC Egypt reconquers Nubia up to the 4th Cataract.

Travel and transport

Most people in Ancient Egypt lived close to the River Nile, so boats provided the quickest and most efficient means of transport.

The Nile flows from south to north, but the wind usually blows from the north. This means that boats can drift down the river with the current, and if they raise their sails the wind will carry them back upstream.

The *hieroglyph*† for 'going upstream' and 'south' showed a ship in sail.

▲

The *hieroglyph* for 'going downstream' and 'north' showed the sail rolled down.

The Nile and the gods

The Nile played such an important part in the lives of the Egyptians that it affected their way of looking at things. For example, they believed that the sun god Re (shown here) travelled by boat across the sky each day. At night he sailed through the Underworld†.

Reed boats

The earliest Egyptian boats were made of reeds bound together. People continued to build this type of boat throughout ancient times, but it was used for short trips only, such as going fishing.

Early reed boat

Wooden boats

By the Old Kingdom, wood (both local and imported) was used for larger boats and for sea-going vessels. Experts have been able to reconstruct a variety of different types from paintings, reliefs† and models left in tombs, and from a few boats that have actually survived. There were different boats for fishing, trading and carrying cargo, as well as barques for funerals and pleasure boats for the rich.

Old Kingdom ▲ fishing boat

Old Kingdom Nile ▲ cargo boat

Old Kingdom sea-going ship

Egyptian ships were constructed so that they could be dismantled easily. This meant they could be carried around the Nile cataracts†, and then reassembled afterwards.

The mast was held up by ropes. It could be lowered and stored when the sail was not needed.

Stern

One or more large oars at the stern were used to steer the ship.

Prow

Many ships had oars as well as sails. This enabled them to travel against the wind if necessary.

Early Egyptian boats were flat-bottomed and had no keel. Instead a huge cable called a hogging truss ran from the prow to the stern. This held the ends up and kept the ship firm.

New Kingdom trading ship

This kind of ship was built in the New Kingdom for trade in the eastern Mediterranean. Most of the space was used for cargo. ▼

Hogging trusses were no longer necessary, as keels began to be used.

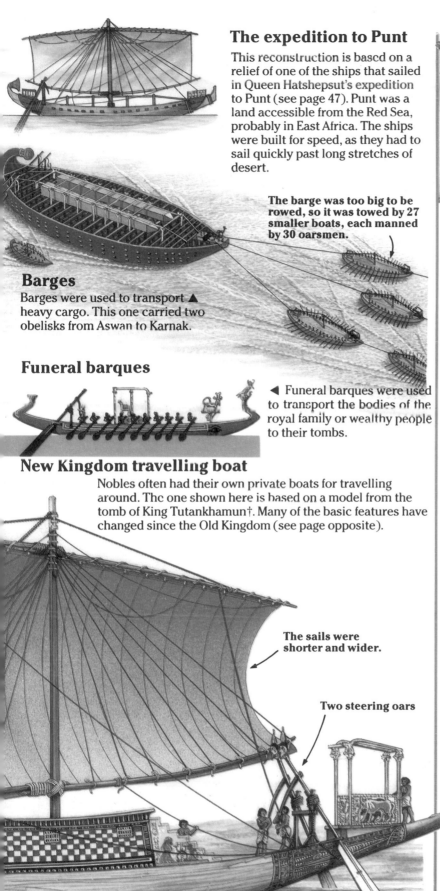

The expedition to Punt

This reconstruction is based on a relief of one of the ships that sailed in Queen Hatshepsut's expedition to Punt (see page 47). Punt was a land accessible from the Red Sea, probably in East Africa. The ships were built for speed, as they had to sail quickly past long stretches of desert.

The barge was too big to be rowed, so it was towed by 27 smaller boats, each manned by 30 oarsmen.

Barges

Barges were used to transport ▲ heavy cargo. This one carried two obelisks from Aswan to Karnak.

Funeral barques

◀ Funeral barques were used to transport the bodies of the royal family or wealthy people to their tombs.

New Kingdom travelling boat

Nobles often had their own private boats for travelling around. The one shown here is based on a model from the tomb of King Tutankhamun†. Many of the basic features have changed since the Old Kingdom (see page opposite).

The sails were shorter and wider.

Two steering oars

The deckhouse was more centrally positioned.

The royal ship of Cheops

This ship was reconstructed from fragments found buried next to the pyramid of Cheops†, the Great Pyramid of Gizah.

Mesopotamian boats

In Mesopotamia boats were also the most important form of transport. The earliest were rafts, reed boats (like the Egyptian one opposite) or coracles (small round rowing boats). ▶

The frame of a coracle was made from reeds and animal hides.

The outside was coated with tar to make it watertight.

Travel on land

Although the Egyptians used the Nile whenever possible, it was sometimes necessary to travel overland. There were no roads as farming land was too precious to waste, and roads would have been washed away annually by the Nile floods (see page 14).

On long desert journeys small loads were carried by donkeys.

Nobles travelled in carrying chairs slung between donkeys, or carried by slaves.

New Kingdom nobles sometimes drove in horse-drawn chariots.

Mining and trade

The Ancient Egyptians were well supplied with a variety of stones and minerals. There were quarries in the deserts within reach of the Nile, and others in Nubia and Sinai. Mining and quarrying expeditions were authorized by the king and financed from taxes. The workforce included expert stonemasons, miners and engineers, but the majority was made up of unskilled men who worked as part of the labour tax which everyone paid to the king. On larger projects criminals and prisoners of war were sometimes used as well. In Sinai local men were often hired.

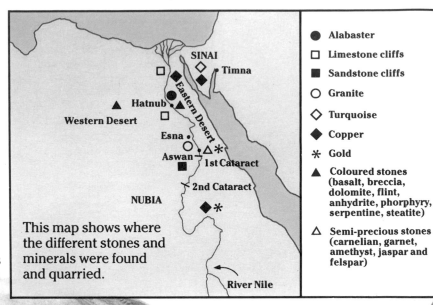

This map shows where the different stones and minerals were found and quarried.

- ● Alabaster
- □ Limestone cliffs
- ■ Sandstone cliffs
- ○ Granite
- ◇ Turquoise
- ◆ Copper
- ✳ Gold
- ▲ Coloured stones (basalt, breccia, dolomite, flint, anhydrite, phorphyry, serpentine, steatite)
- △ Semi-precious stones (carnelian, garnet, amethyst, jaspar and felspar)

A mining camp

There is evidence of Egyptian gold mines in the Eastern Desert and of copper and turquoise mines in Sinai dating back to the Old Kingdom. This reconstruction shows a copper mining camp at Timna in Sinai. Egyptian mining engineers appear to have been highly skilled. Vertical shafts up to 70m (230ft) deep led into long tunnels cut deep into the cliffs. The shafts acted as air vents and connected the tunnels to each other.

Stone barracks for the men

Storehouses

The miners dug the copper ore from the cliff sides.

Cattle stores

The copper was beaten into pieces shaped like oxhides.

The copper ore was carried away in panniers on donkeys.

Soldiers were usually sent to the camps to protect the workmen and the metal from bandits and hostile bedouin†.

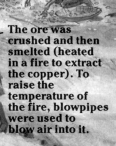

Egyptian maps described the route an expedition should follow, and included details such as distances, the positions of wells, and areas frequented by nomads†. This is a New Kingdom map of gold mines at Wadi Hammamat.

The ore was crushed and then smelted (heated in a fire to extract the copper). To raise the temperature of the fire, blowpipes were used to blow air into it.

Egyptian trade

Egypt was well placed for trade with both Africa and Asia. Crossing frontiers in search of metals and other goods often involved the Egyptians in clashes with the local inhabitants, so trade became linked with foreign policy. One of the main aims of Egyptian policy was to protect trade routes and supplies, and this led to the conquest and occupation of places such as Nubia and Sinai, especially in the New Kingdom. Foreign trade was normally under the control of the king, although temples and merchants were sometimes allowed to trade abroad too.

Syrian trading ship being unloaded

Important officials were put in charge of despatching and receiving trading missions.

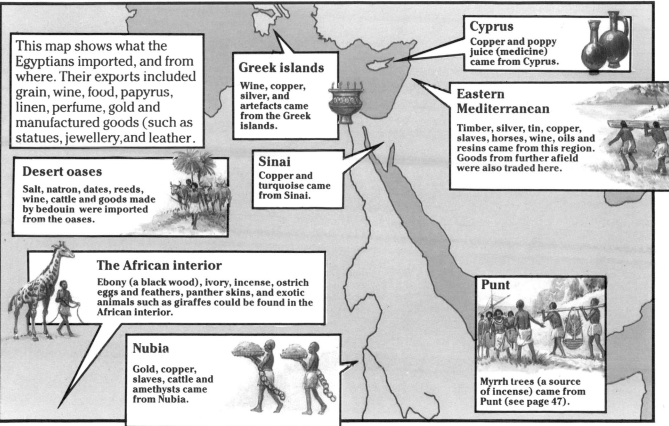

This map shows what the Egyptians imported, and from where. Their exports included grain, wine, food, papyrus, linen, perfume, gold and manufactured goods (such as statues, jewellery, and leather.

Greek islands

Wine, copper, silver, and artefacts came from the Greek islands.

Cyprus

Copper and poppy juice (medicine) came from Cyprus.

Eastern Mediterranean

Timber, silver, tin, copper, slaves, horses, wine, oils and resins came from this region. Goods from further afield were also traded here.

Sinai

Copper and turquoise came from Sinai.

Desert oases

Salt, natron, dates, reeds, wine, cattle and goods made by bedouin were imported from the oases.

The African interior

Ebony (a black wood), ivory, incense, ostrich eggs and feathers, panther skins, and exotic animals such as giraffes could be found in the African interior.

Punt

Myrrh trees (a source of incense) came from Punt (see page 47).

Nubia

Gold, copper, slaves, cattle and amethysts came from Nubia.

Buying and selling

Although a few surviving tomb scenes show small market stalls, little is known about shopping in Egypt. Craftsmen probably sold their goods from the front rooms of their houses or at royal or temple workshops. The Egyptians did not use money. They exchanged goods which were agreed to be of approximately equal value. For example, two copper vases might be considered to be worth five linen tunics. A system was later developed by which the value was assessed in copper weights called *deben*. Goods of an equal value were exchanged. Sometimes, people actually gave the *deben* instead. However a proper coinage system was not developed until the 7th century BC in Lydia (Asia Minor).

The Egyptians used scales and standard weights. This painting shows gold rings being weighed with a weight shaped like a bull's head.

33

The government of Egypt

The Egyptians believed that the position of king of Egypt had been introduced by the gods at the time of the creation of the world. The kings were thought to be descended from the sun god Re*, who had been the first king of Egypt. Ordinary people believed they could communicate with the gods through the king. The king was thought to be so holy that it was considered impolite to refer to him directly. People therefore referred to him indirectly as 'Great House' (or palace). The Egyptian words were *per-o*, from which we get the word 'pharaoh'. The king had five official titles, the first and oldest of which was 'The Horus'*.

The Egyptians believed that when the king was on his throne, wearing his royal regalia, the spirit of Horus entered him. During Dynasty XVIII, the queen became closely associated with Horus's wife, the goddess Hathor.

The king's crowns

The king's crown, the Double Crown, combined the White Crown of Upper Egypt and the Red Crown of Lower Egypt. The king was often described as 'The Lord of the Two Lands'.

Double Crown

Red Crown   **White Crown**

This jewelled headband, known as the royal diadem, shows the vulture and cobra goddesses (see page 9) who were thought to protect the king. The goddesses are referred to in another of the king's titles 'He of the Two Ladies'.

The king's role

The king had absolute power. He also had a number of duties. It was his responsibility to rule justly and to maintain *ma'at* (the order, harmony and balance of the Universe). The king played a part in every aspect of life.

◀ The king was responsible for the harvest and the irrigation system. People believed he could influence the weather and keep animals and plants fertile.

Government, law, ▶ trade and foreign policy were all directed by the king.

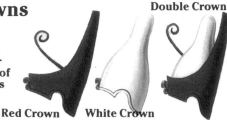

◀ The king led his armies into battle.

The king

The king was seen as the ▶ mediator betwen the people and the gods, and was therefore the head of the cults † of all the gods.

Osiris

The royal succession

Marriage between close relatives, including brother and sister, was usual within the Egyptian royal family (although not for ordinary people). It was seen as a way of maintaining the purity of royal blood. The king had many wives, but usually only one queen. She was the eldest daughter of the former king and queen, and was known as the Royal Heiress. The king could nominate any of his sons as his successor (although the queen's sons were the most eligible). However in order to confirm his claim the boy would marry the next Royal Heiress (the queen's eldest daughter), who would be his sister or half-sister.

Ceremonies

There were a number of ceremonies which were designed to keep the king in power and protect him from enemies. One important one was *Heb Sed*, which was supposed to renew the king's strength and powers. It was often held after he had reigned for 30 years, although the king could choose to hold it at any time to indicate that he was making a new start to his rule.

This relief† shows the king running. This was one of the rituals of the *Heb Sed* festival.

*For more about Re, Horus and other Egyptian gods and goddesses, see pages 20-21.

The organization of the government

The Pharaoh

Although government policy was decided by the Pharaoh, he delegated the day to day management of affairs to officials and departments of state.

The most important officials were the two Viziers. One was in charge of Upper Egypt and was based in Thebes. The other, in charge of Lower Egypt, was based in Memphis. Egypt was divided up into rural districts, controlled by governors, and towns, controlled by mayors.

Each Vizier, governor and mayor had a staff of officials, messengers and scribes†. They were responsible for carrying out the orders of central government and collecting taxes. The scribes kept the records, which helped the system run efficiently.

There was an official in charge of each state department – the Treasury, the Granaries, Royal Works, Cattle and Foreign Affairs.

Vizier of Upper Egypt

All official positions were duplicated, with one set for Upper Egypt and another for Lower Egypt.

Vizier of Lower Egypt

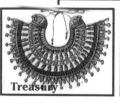

Officials

Scribes

Messenger

Treasury — **Royal Works** — **Granaries** — **Cattle** — **Foreign Affairs**

Taxation

The Egyptian government imposed a number of different taxes on its people. As there was no money, taxes were paid 'in kind' (with produce or work). The Vizier controlled the taxation system through the departments of state. The departments had to report daily on the amount of stock available, and how much was expected in the future.

Tribute† from conquered peoples ▶ **played an important part, especially in the New Kingdom. These tribute bearers are from Syria, Nubia and the Sinai Desert.**

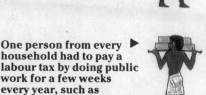

Syrian   **Nubians**   **Bedouin from Sinai**   **Nubians**

Traders paid duty on imports ▲ **and exports.**

There was a tax on land ▶ **which was paid in grain and other produce. It was based on the estimated yield of the crop (see page 15).**

Craftsmen had to ▶ **pay taxes on the goods they produced.**

Hunters and ▶ **fishermen paid taxes on produce from the river, the marshes and the desert.**

One person from every ▶ **household had to pay a labour tax by doing public work for a few weeks every year, such as repairing canals or mining (see page 32).**

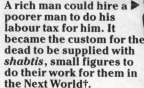

A rich man could hire a ▶ **poorer man to do his labour tax for him. It became the custom for the dead to be supplied with *shabtis*, small figures to do their work for them in the Next World†.**

35

Costume, jewellery and cosmetics

Egyptian fashions changed very little throughout ancient times. Most clothes were made of linen, which varied from a coarse weave to a fine semi-transparent material. In winter, the Egyptians may have worn wool too, but it was regarded as impure and so has not been mentioned in texts or found in tombs. The clothes shown in tomb paintings were usually white, but this may have been simply because white was considered to be pure or because it was used for special occasions. There is evidence that the Egyptians wore coloured fabrics too.

Many people kept their hair short, because of the climate. Nobles tended to have longer hair or wear wigs (straight, plaited or curled). There were a variety of preparations for the hair – henna (a vegetable dye) to colour it, and mixtures to prevent baldness, dandruff and grey hair.

The Old and Middle Kingdoms

The basic costume for a ▶ man was a kilt, made from a piece of linen wrapped around the body and tied at the waist.

For a woman the basic costume was a straight dress held up by two straps.

Noblemen wore pleated kilts in a variety of styles. Older men, particularly important officials, sometimes wore longer kilts. ▼

Wraps and cloaks were worn in winter. These are very rarely shown in tomb paintings, presumably because good weather was expected in the Next World†.

When doing heavy, hot, dirty jobs, men wore a kilt or a loincloth and women a short skirt.

◀ Children usually ran around naked during the summer. They sometimes had their heads shaved, except for a long plait, called the 'lock of youth'.

Padded hairstyle

Noblewomen also wore beaded dresses. The beads may have been sewn on, or strung together and worn over the dress. In the Middle Kingdom it was fashionable to pad out the hair or decorate it with ornaments.

Some clothes were decorated with stripes, squares or diamond shapes, or made up of overlapping pieces of material. This servant girl is wearing a patterned dress.

The New Kingdom

By the time of the New Kingdom, styles became much more elaborate, particularly for special occasions. Clothes were looser and more flowing and arranged with numbers of pleats.

A nobleman ▶ sometimes wore a long robe over his kilt. Loose, thin cloaks were also fashionable.

Belt

◀ Noblewomen wore flowing pleated dresses and shawls. The shawl was made from a single piece of cloth folded round the body and knotted under the breasts.

New Kingdom hairstyles were often long, with lots of plaits and curls. ▼

Some queens are ▶ shown wearing a ceremonial costume apparently decorated with feathers, like the garment on this bronze statue of Queen Karomama. Kings also appear to have worn feathered cloaks.

Masses of small sequins were found in the tomb of Tutankhamun†. Each one was pierced with two holes, which suggests that they may have been sewn on to clothes as decoration.

Shoes and gloves

People often went barefoot, although they had sandals made of reeds or leather for formal occasions. Nobles had highly decorated sandals, like the ones on the right which belonged to Tutankhamun. The gloves shown here were also found in his tomb, although gloves were never shown in paintings.

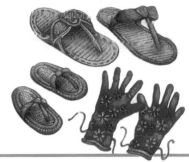

Wigs

Wigs were worn by both sexes at parties and official functions. Special boxes with a stand inside were used to store the wigs while they were not in use.

Wig with hair ornaments ▲

Toiletries and cosmetics

Cleanliness was important to the Egyptians. Most people washed themselves in the river or with a jug and basin at home. Rich people had rooms where they took showers by getting a servant to pour water over them. The water drained away through a pipe into the garden. A cleansing cream made from oil, lime and perfume was used instead of soap. People rubbed themselves daily with oil, to prevent the hot sun from drying and cracking their skin. Razors and tweezers were used to remove body hair and there were preparations to cure spots and eliminate body odours. Both sexes wore perfume and eye make-up.

Cosmetic chest

Malachite (copper ore) or galena (lead ore) was ground in a palette and mixed with oil to make eyepaint called kohl. This was kept in jars and put on with a small stick.

Make-up box

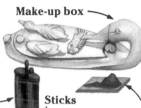

Henna was used to paint the nails, and possibly the palms of the hands and the soles of the feet too.

Perfume jar →

Cosmetic jars → **Sticks**

Mirrors were made of highly polished copper or silver, not glass.

Red ochre (a type of clay) was ground and mixed with water, and applied to the cheeks and the lips.

Jewellery

It appears that everyone in Egypt wore jewellery. For the rich there were beautiful pieces made of gold, silver or electrum (gold mixed with silver), inlaid with semi-precious stones and coloured glass. Poorer people wore copper or faience (made by heating powdered quartz).

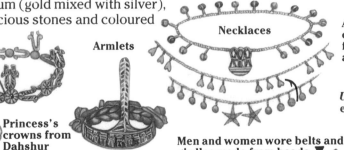

Necklaces

Armlets

A pectoral was a large piece of jewellery made in the form of a picture and hung around the neck.

Udjat eye†

Princess's crowns from Dahshur ◄ (Dynasty XII)

Men and women wore belts and girdles made from beads. ▼

Bead collars were fastened by cords at the back of the neck. ▼

Pendant

Earrings were introduced in the New Kingdom. ▼

Ankh †

Pectoral of Princess Sit-Hathor →

Many pieces of jewellery contained amulets † and sacred symbols, such as the scarab beetle.

Bracelets

Anklets

Rings

Scarab beetle †

Entertainment

Evidence of how the Egyptians spent their spare time comes from paintings and objects left in tombs. There were no theatres, but dramatized performances held at temples told tales of the lives of the gods. Religious festivals and royal processions also provided colourful spectacles. However, one of the most important sources of sport and relaxation was the river.

The river

Many tomb paintings show noblemen catching fish, waterfowl and river animals in the marshes. They used harpoons to catch the fish, whereas peasants who fished for a living used large nets.

Wealthy families often went on outings on the river in small papyrus† boats.

A favourite game among peasant boatmen seems to have been a contest between two teams armed with long poles. Each team tried to knock the other into the river.

Swimming in the Nile was the natural way to cool off in the heat, although people had to choose their bathing places very carefully to avoid crocodiles.

Cats were sometimes taken on hunting expeditions. They may have been used to flush out the birds.

Hunting crocodiles and hippopotamuses was a very dangerous pastime. A team of hunters and boatmen was needed to harpoon the animals and bring them ashore with ropes and nets.

Hunting in the desert

Hunting desert animals was a favourite pastime for noblemen. At first they hunted on foot, but from the New Kingdom onwards they also used horses and chariots. The Egyptians usually hunted antelope, hare, fox and hyena, although paintings and reliefs show kings tackling bulls and lions too. By Dynasty XVIII, the empire had expanded and new animals, such as rhinoceros and elephant, became available. This golden fan shows Tutankhamun† hunting ostriches.

Ostrich feathers would have been used for the plumes of the fan.

The Egyptians had hounds that were specially bred for hunting. They had long legs, pointed muzzles and curling tails.

38

Parties, music and dancing

Wealthy Egyptians often entertained lavishly, giving large parties with plenty of food and drink. Groups of professional singers, musicians, dancers, jugglers and acrobats were hired to entertain the guests. Paintings and reliefs demonstrate many different styles of dance, some of which are shown here.

This painting shows servants offering the guests flowers and cones of perfumed fat to put on their heads. These had a cooling and refreshing effect as the fat melted.

The Egyptians loved music and singing. This wall-painting shows some of the instruments they played, which included lutes, lyres, harps and several types of flute and pipes.

Harp | Lute | Double flute made of two reed stalks | Lyre

Games

Egyptians from all backgrounds appear to have played games with counters on boards, although the rules have not survived. Gaming boards made of ebony, ivory and gold have been found in royal tombs. Most ordinary boards would have been made of mud or local wood.

A game called *senet* may have been the most popular. This board was found in a tomb.

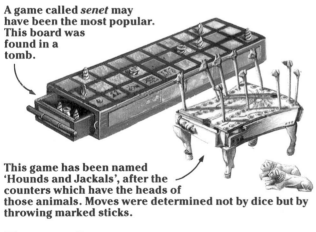

This game has been named 'Hounds and Jackals', after the counters which have the heads of those animals. Moves were determined not by dice but by throwing marked sticks.

Pets and zoos

The Egyptians kept a variety of pets, including dogs, cats, monkeys and geese. Small, short-legged breeds of dogs often appear in tomb scenes, and their collars were sometimes buried with their owners. References to pet cats date from the Middle Kingdom. Cats are sometimes shown at parties, sitting beneath their owners' chairs. Some pharaohs of Dynasty XVIII seem to have collected exotic animals and even set up their own private zoos.

Toys

A number of toys, like the ones shown here, have been found in children's graves. Some of them were quite elaborate, with moving parts.

Ivory dog with moving jaws ▼

Painted doll ▶

Wooden ▶ animal

Balls ▶

Dancing figures ▲ made of ivory

Wooden horse on wheels ▶

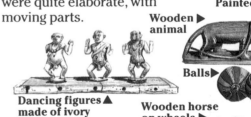

Some tomb paintings show children playing what look like team games.

Mesopotamian pastimes

Archaeological evidence suggests that Mesopotamian sports and pastimes were similar to those of the Egyptians.

◀ A silver lyre found at Ur

A board game from the royal tombs at Ur (see page 7) ▶

The law

Most of the surviving information about the Egyptian legal system dates from the New Kingdom onwards. Egyptian laws covered every aspect of life. Records were kept of each law that had been passed and any judgements that had been made in previous cases. The Egyptians' system appears to have been highly regarded by their contemporaries in the ancient world. King Darius† of Persia asked for translations of Egyptian laws to be made for him.

◀ Ma'at (shown here) was the goddess of truth and justice. She is sometimes shown in paintings standing behind the king, who was the head of the legal system on Earth. Judges often became her priests.

The Medjay used hunters and dogs to help them track down criminals. Suspects may have been rounded up before a trial and locked in an unused storeroom of a temple. There do not appear to have been any prisons.

The Medjay

The Medjay was originally a Nubian tribe that came to Egypt as mercenary soldiers. It gradually evolved into a peace-keeping force, which was joined by native Egyptians. By the New Kingdom, there were groups of Medjay stationed in all major Egyptian towns. Their job was to keep law and order, catch criminals, and to guard the frontiers and cemeteries. The Medjay had an intimate knowledge of local matters, which helped in dealing with crimes.

The law courts

The day to day running of law and order was under the control of the law courts. Justice was supposed to be available for all, not just the rich, and Egyptians regularly took each other to court. There do not seem to have been any barristers, so people had to speak for themselves. Each town had its own court, called a *kenbet*. The judges,

who were chosen from important local men, also travelled to country areas. Then came the higher courts (called the Court of Listeners), under the supervision of the district governor. Above them were two Great Courts (one each for Upper and Lower Egypt), presided over by the Vizier. This is a reconstruction of a court scene.

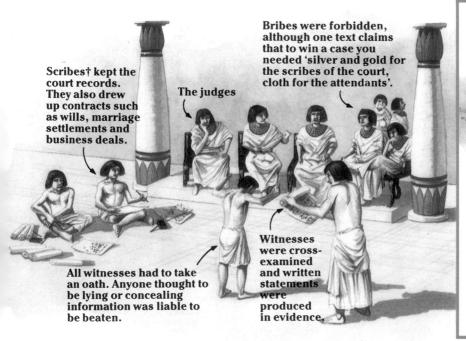

Scribes† kept the court records. They also drew up contracts such as wills, marriage settlements and business deals.

The judges

Bribes were forbidden, although one text claims that to win a case you needed 'silver and gold for the scribes of the court, cloth for the attendants'.

All witnesses had to take an oath. Anyone thought to be lying or concealing information was liable to be beaten.

Witnesses were cross-examined and written statements were produced in evidence.

Verdicts and punishments

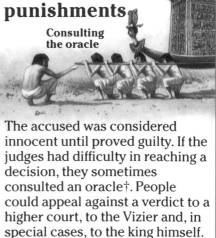

Consulting the oracle

The accused was considered innocent until proved guilty. If the judges had difficulty in reaching a decision, they sometimes consulted an oracle†. People could appeal against a verdict to a higher court, to the Vizier and, in special cases, to the king himself. Punishments included fines, flogging, hard labour, mutilation, exile or death. There do not appear to have been any prisons.

Medicine

Egyptian doctors were highly regarded throughout the Middle East and some travelled abroad at the request of foreign princes. A New Kingdom tomb painting shows a foreign prince bringing his whole family to Egypt to consult a doctor.

Doctors may have been trained by other doctors in their families, although there were probably medical schools too. There is evidence of at least one school for midwives. Most doctors worked in the community as general practitioners. Others worked in temples, or as army surgeons or specialist consultants. The best doctors were appointed as court physicians.

This Egyptian doctor is treating a Syrian princess.

Egyptian doctors understood quite a lot about how the body worked. They also had some knowledge of the nervous system and the effects of injury on the spine. They knew that an injury to the right side of the head affected the left side of the body, and vice versa. Although they may not have fully understood the circulation system, they knew that the heart pumped blood through the body. They described the pulse as 'speaking the messages of the heart'.

This is the mummified head of Ramesses II†. Modern medical examination of other mummies† has revealed information about ancient diseases.

Diseases and remedics

The Egyptians had specialist medical textbooks on diagnosis, treatment and medicines, as well as specialist books on anatomy, women's diseases, dentistry, surgery and veterinary science. Copies of parts of these books have survived, and Egyptian doctors consulted them when treating diseases and preparing remedies. Experts cannot be sure how effective all Egyptian medicines were, but some of the ingredients that can be identified would certainly have worked.

Egyptian surgical instruments

Papyrus scroll

Egyptian doctors were taught first to observe the symptoms, then to ask questions, inspect, smell, feel and probe. They were instructed to make detailed notes of their observations, treatments and results, for use in future cases. Evidence suggests that doctors were prepared to admit when they did not know, or were not sure, how to cure something. Operations were occasionally performed. Surgeons cleaned their blades in fire before use and kept the patient and the surroundings as clean as possible.

Some patients undergoing surgery were given a pain-killer which may have been opium. It was imported from Cyprus in jugs like these.

The gods of medicine

Religion played a part in the treatment of illness, especially when dealing with psychological problems. Prayers were always said during a treatment, and were probably seen as more important when the illness was very serious. Several Egyptian deities were particularly associated with medicine and healing: Thoth, Sekhmet, Isis and Imhotep*.

This *stela*† was meant to protect against bites and stings.

People often went to the temples of these deities to be cured. Attached to the temples were doctors, who were usually priests too. In some cases the patient was allowed to spend the night in a room near the sanctuary. People believed that the patient might be cured by a miracle†. If not, he or she might have a dream on which the doctor would base the treatment.

See page 12 for more about Imhotep, and pages 20-21 for more about the other Egyptian gods and goddesses.

Early civilization in China

China is isolated geographically, cut off from the rest of the world by sea, mountains, and the vast freezing plains of the Steppes in central Asia. As far as we know, China had no direct contact with the West before the 2nd century BC. It therefore developed very differently from other ancient cultures. Remains of early people have been found dating back to 30,000BC.

There is evidence of farming communities by the Huang Ho River from about 5000BC. This is known as the Yangshao culture. Farmers grew millet (a kind of cereal), fruit, nuts and vegetables and kept pigs and dogs. Farming also developed along the Yangtze River, where rice was cultivated from about 4000BC. In the Longshan period (c.2500BC), settlements were better organized. Farmers kept chickens, cattle, sheep and goats, and buffalo for ploughing and transport.

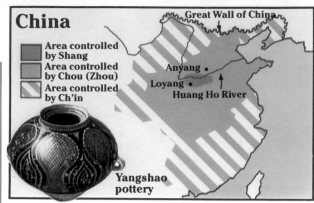

China

Area controlled by Shang
Area controlled by Chou (Zhou)
Area controlled by Ch'in

Great Wall of China
Anyang
Loyang
Huang Ho River

Yangshao pottery

Yangshao settlement

The first dynasties

After the farming cultures, China was ruled by a series of dynasties†. The first of these, the Hsia (Xia)* Dynasty, is traditionally said to have begun in about 2205BC, but little evidence of it has been found. In about 1766BC the Shang Dynasty began in what is now Henan province. The Shang eventually controlled land as far south as the Yangtze River. They moved their capital several times, lastly to a place called Anyang.

The Bronze Age in China began with the Shang Dynasty. Elaborate vessels like this were used for religious ceremonies.

Writing

Shang rulers employed men who predicted the future by scorching bones and tortoise shells until they cracked. They then interpreted the 'messages' revealed by the cracks. Oracle bones contain the first known examples of Chinese writing. The script was difficult to learn, as it had several thousand characters, each representing a word. Variants of many of these symbols remain in use in Chinese script today.

Oracle bone

*The traditional spelling is shown with the modern spelling in brackets.

The Chou Dynasty

At the end of the 11th century BC the Shang were conquered by a people called the Chou (Zhou)*, who extended the territory further. It was divided into smaller areas, some ruled by the king, others by appointed leaders. During this period there were many wars and political changes.

Chariots were used in battle. These chariot ornaments were found in a grave near Loyang, the Chou capital.

Trade

The Chou period was one of economic growth and increased trade. The Chinese had goods that were unavailable elsewhere, such as silk, which was made from the thread produced by the larvae of certain moths. By the 1st century BC silk was exported as far as the Roman empire. Other Chinese exports included semi-precious stones (especially jade), porcelain and spices.

Silk funeral banner

Life in a Chou city

Excavations at ancient Chinese sites reveal large walled cities with areas set aside for rulers, temples and cemeteries. Additional evidence, such as models placed in graves, tells us what a Chinese city might have looked like.

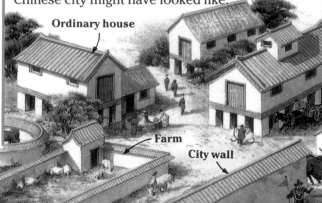

Ordinary house
Farm
City wall

The rise of the Ch'in Dynasty

During the 8th century BC Chou authority declined. The smaller states fought each other for supremacy and in the 5th century BC seven major kingdoms emerged. For the next 250 years they were constantly at war. (This is known as the Warring States Period.) Finally one kingdom, the Ch'in, dominated the others. The first Ch'in emperor, Shi-huang-ti, succeeded in uniting his territory and improving law and administration. Ch'in is the origin of the word 'China'.

Shi-huang-ti standardized coinage so that everyone used the same money all over the empire. Coins had holes in the middle so that they could be threaded on cords.

Religion and burial

The Chinese had many gods. They also believed very firmly in life after death and in the power of their ancestors. They buried food and personal belongings with the dead, often in magnificent tombs. In the Shang period slaves and animals were killed and placed in royal tombs with their masters. This custom later died out and models of attendants were used instead.

A 2nd century BC prince and his wife were buried in jade suits. Jade was thought to preserve the body.

Shi-huang-ti was buried with thousands of life-size model warriors made of terracotta†.

Philosophers and prophets

The Chinese believed that their rulers were descended from a god called Shang ti, who granted dynasties the right to rule, and could withdraw it at any time. This idea helped them to account for changes of dynasty.

In the 6th century BC other beliefs grew up. The prophet Kong zi (shown here), known in the West as Confucius, lived in a period of warfare. He believed that peace would only be restored if people obeyed a strict code of behaviour. Confucianism later became the basis of Chinese social and political conduct.

The prophet Lao-zi founded Taoism. He taught that if people were in tune with the natural world they would behave correctly.

Warriors and weapons

Many Shang and Chou warriors fought in chariots, but during the Warring States Period there were increasing numbers of footsoldiers, and armies contained up to one million men. Iron working was introduced in the 6th century BC and was used to make tools and armour. After the invention of the crossbow in about 450BC, soldiers were issued with iron armour to protect them.

Under the Chou, many nobles had built walls to defend their territory. In 214BC, Shi-huang-ti had them joined and extended to keep out the hostile Hsung nu tribe (known as Huns). The result was an immense frontier about 3000km (1865 miles) long, known as the Great Wall of China.

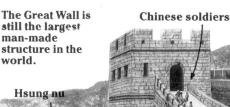

The Great Wall is still the largest man-made structure in the world.

Chinese soldiers

Hsung nu

Key dates

c.5000BC Yangshao culture: farming settlements are established by the Huang Ho River.

c.2500BC Longshan culture

c.2205-1766BC Dates traditionally given for the Hsia (Xia) Dynasty

1766-1027BC Shang Dynasty

1027-221BC Chou (Zhou) Dynasty

c.700BC Hostile tribes invade from the north.

c.722-481BC Chou royal power declines. Small states fight each other (the 'Spring and Autumn Period').

481-221BC Seven major states destroy each other in struggles for power (the Warring States Period).

221BC Unification of China by the first Ch'in emperor, Shi-huang-ti.

Migrations in the Middle East

In about 2000BC, groups of people known by modern scholars as Indo-Europeans drifted into the Middle East. Some settled there; some moved on. They probably came from the great plains that stretch from central Europe eastwards into south Russia. Although their cultures often differed, their languages were all related, having apparently evolved from a single common tongue. Most modern European languages are descended from that original Indo-European language, as are Iranian, Armenian and Sanskrit (the ancient literary language of India).

The Hittites

The Hittites were Indo-Europeans who settled in Anatolia (part of modern Turkey) in about 2000BC and were probably united under one kingdom in about 1740BC. The Hittites expanded into north Syria and conquered Babylon (see page 76) in about 1595BC. During the Hittite New Kingdom (c.1450-1200BC), they were one of Egypt's most dangerous enemies. They built up a huge empire, but it collapsed with the coming of the Sea Peoples (see page 71).

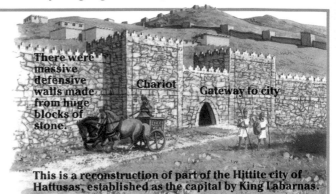

There were massive defensive walls made from huge blocks of stone.

Chariot

Gateway to city

This is a reconstruction of part of the Hittite city of Hattusas, established as the capital by King Labarnas.

Migration of Indo-Europeans

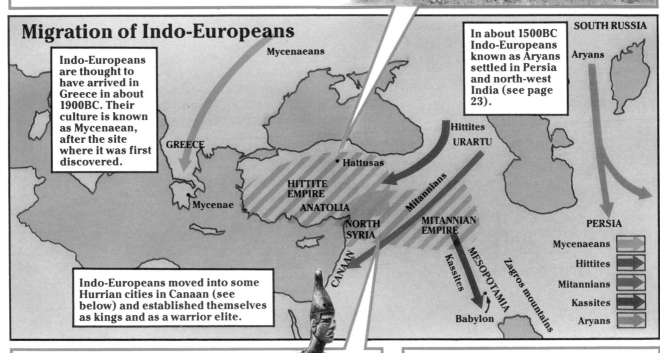

Indo-Europeans are thought to have arrived in Greece in about 1900BC. Their culture is known as Mycenaean, after the site where it was first discovered.

In about 1500BC Indo-Europeans known as Aryans settled in Persia and north-west India (see page 23).

Indo-Europeans moved into some Hurrian cities in Canaan (see below) and established themselves as kings and as a warrior elite.

SOUTH RUSSIA

Mycenaeans

Aryans

Hittites
URARTU

GREECE

Mycenae

Hattusas

HITTITE EMPIRE
ANATOLIA

NORTH SYRIA

CANAAN

Mitannians

MITANNIAN EMPIRE

Kassites

MESOPOTAMIA

Zagros mountains

Babylon

PERSIA

Mycenaeans
Hittites
Mitannians
Kassites
Aryans

The Mitannians

The Mitannians were Indo-Europeans who settled in northern Mesopotamia. In about 1500BC they united the Hurrian kingdoms under their rule. Between about 1450BC and 1390BC they built up an empire from the Zagros mountains to the Mediterranean. The Mitannians were keen horsemen and wrote books on horse management. Although originally rivals of the Egyptians, they made peace in about 1440BC. The kingdom broke up in about 1370BC after an attack by Hittites.

A Mitannian king

The Hurrians

The Hurrians first appeared in Mesopotamia in the 3rd millennium BC. Little is known about their origins, although they may have come from Urartu (modern Armenia), and they were neither Sumerian nor Semitic. They established kingdoms in northern Mesopotamia and later united with the Mitannians. During the 2nd millennium BC they formed an aristocratic caste† in many cities in Canaan, ruling the Amorites and native Canaanites.

Horses

Horses were native to the plains of Europe and south Russia and were probably first

domesticated in about 4000BC, for use as work animals. They first appeared in the Middle East just before 2000BC, but were kept as expensive pets. Later the Indo-Europeans introduced the idea of using horses to pull war chariots. This had an effect on warfare, as it meant new military skills were needed.

Horses were used to pull chariots, like this Egyptian war chariot. They were rarely ridden.

The Kassites

The Kassites were neither Semitic nor Indo-European. They are thought to have come from the Zagros mountains, east of Babylon. Some settled in Babylon; others founded a state on the frontier. After the Hittites attacked Babylon (see opposite), the Kassites took over and set up a dynasty†

Kassite decorated brickwork

Key dates

c.2000BC Indo-Europeans drift into Middle East. Hittites settle in Anatolia.

c.1900BC Mycenaeans settle in Greece.

c.1680-1650BC Rule of King Labarnas; he is regarded by the Hittites as the founder of their kingdom.

c.1640-1552BC Second Intermediate Period in Egypt.

c.1595BC Hittites conquer Babylon and destroy the Amorite kingdom (see page 25).

c.1570-1158BC Kassite dynasty rules in Babylon.

c.1500BC Aryans settle in Persia.

c.1500BC Mitannians move into northern Mesopotamia and unite Hurrian kingdoms under their rule.

c.1450-1390BC Mitannians conquer a huge empire.

c.1450-1200BC Hittite New Kingdom

c.1440BC Mitannians make peace treaty with the Egyptians.

c.1380BC Accession of King Shuppiluliuma†, one of the greatest Hittite kings. He overthrows the Mitannian empire and captures northern provinces of the Egyptian empire in Syria.

c.1285BC Hittite coalition clashes with Ramesses II† at Kadesh.

c.1275BC Ramesses II makes a peace treaty with Hittite king, Hattusilis III, and marries his daughter.

c.1196BC Destruction of the Hittite empire by the Sea Peoples.

Egypt in the Second Intermediate Period

The collapse of the Middle Kingdom (see page 27) was caused by the invasion of a Semitic people, called Hyksos, from across the eastern frontier. After a period of fighting and destruction, the Hyksos adopted the Egyptian language and culture. They ruled Lower Egypt and northern Upper Egypt, as Dynasties XV and XVI, from their capital, Avaris.

Meanwhile, the southern part of Upper Egypt was ruled from Thebes by the Egyptian kings of Dynasty XVII. Although nominally independent, they were dominated by the Hyksos and had to pay tribute to them. The Egyptian kingdom was

The Hyksos introduced horses and chariots into Egypt.

poor, both culturally and economically, and cut off from foreign trade. However, in about 1600BC came the first signs of revival. The kings started restoring damaged monuments at Abydos and Coptos and encouraged the copying of old manuscripts. Amun*, the patron god of Dynasty XII, became the symbol of an Egyptian resistance movement against the Hyksos.

Tao and the hippos

The Egyptians had a sacred rite which involved harpooning a male hippopotamus, the symbol of Set*, the god of trouble. The Hyksos worshipped Set as the 'benefactor of mankind', so they took the ritual as a deliberate insult and a declaration of hostility. On one occasion, Apophis†, king of the Hyksos, complained to the Theban king, Tao II†, that he was being kept awake in Avaris by the hippos in Tao's pool in Thebes, over 850km (500 miles) away.

Egyptian hippo made of faience†

War with the Hyksos

War followed between the Thebans and the Hyksos, during which Tao was killed. His elder son, Kamose†, became king and extended the Egyptian frontiers as far as the Fayum. Kamose died young and was succeeded by his young brother, Ahmose†, who drove out the Hyksos and became the first king of Dynasty XVIII. This began the New Kingdom (see pages 46-47).

Battle axe belonging to Ahmose

The early New Kingdom

The New Kingdom (1552-1069BC) was the great age of warrior pharaohs and of the Egyptian empire. The occupation of the Hyksos (see page 45) had left the Egyptians with a new aggressive spirit. This drove them to conquer territory beyond their traditional frontiers and to build up the greatest empire of the day (see map, page 81). This brought them into direct conflict with other imperial powers, such as the Mitannians and the Hittites (see page 44).

Some kings put on special displays to demonstrate their military skill. Amenhotep II used to shoot arrows through copper targets while he galloped past them in his chariot.

The New Kingdom kings took on a more active military role than most earlier kings had done. They were personally responsible for planning campaign strategy and individual battle tactics, and they fought in battle alongside their soldiers. Military skills now formed an important part of the education of young princes. Friendships developed between kings and some officers. In peacetime these men were given top jobs in the government.

The age of queens

During the New Kingdom a number of queens appear to have had political influence. Teti-sheri†, the mother of Tao II† and grandmother of Kamose† and Ahmose I†, seems to have had an important role during the wars of independence.

Her daughter, Ahhotep I†, was regent† during the minority† rule of her son, Ahmose. There is evidence that she led her troops herself during a rebellion. A necklace of 'golden flies', an award for gallantry on the battlefield, was found in her tomb.

Ahmes Nefertari†, sister-wife of Ahmose, acted as regent for her son, Amenhotep I. When he died without heirs, she helped her daughter's husband, Tuthmosis I, to become king.

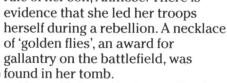

Ahmes Nefertari was later worshipped as a goddess. This painting shows her with a black face, which symbolized fertility.

Hatshepsut (1490-1468BC)

The most remarkable of all the queens was Hatshepsut. As the only surviving child of Queen Ahmose, Hatshepsut became Royal Heiress† and married her half-brother, Tuthmosis II. He died young, leaving two daughters by Hatshepsut, and a son, Tuthmosis III, by his concubine† Isis. Although still only a child, the boy became king and married his elder half-sister, Neferure. Hatshepsut was made regent, presumably because Isis was regarded as unsuitable.

Hatshepsut's family tree

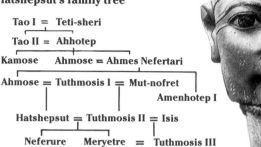

```
Tao I  =  Teti-sheri

Tao II  =  Ahhotep

Kamose      Ahmose = Ahmes Nefertari

Ahmose = Tuthmosis I = Mut-nofret
                              Amenhotep I

Hatshepsut = Tuthmosis II = Isis

Neferure    Meryetre  =  Tuthmosis III
```

About 18 months later, Hatshepsut and her friends staged a coup during a temple ceremony at Karnak. As the statue of Amun* was carried past her it became so heavy that the priests sank to their knees. The oracle† declared this to be a sign that Amun wanted her to rule. The majority of courtiers appear to have supported this, despite the fact that there had been child kings before. As the ruler was believed to be the god Horus incarnate on earth, he was by definition male. So Hatshepsut was crowned 'king', rather than queen. Official statues show her in men's clothes and inscriptions usually refer to her as 'His Majesty'.

According to the propaganda, she was actually the daughter of Amun. He had fallen in love with Ahmose and, disguised as Tuthmosis I, become Hatshepsut's father.

Hatshepsut's parents, Tuthmosis I and Ahmose ▶

Hatshepsut ruled successfully for about 20 years, though evidence of her reign is scarce as her official inscriptions were later wiped out. She appears to have restored many buildings destroyed by the Hyksos and extended the temple of Amun at Karnak. It was once thought that, as a woman, she could not fight and so pursued a policy of peace. However evidence from the inscriptions of her courtiers suggests that she may have fought in person in Nubia and in the East.

For more about Amun and other Egyptian deities, see pages 20-21.

The expedition to Punt

One of Hatshepsut's achievements was to send a successful expedition to Punt, to bring back myrrh trees, which were highly valued by the Egyptians. The land of Punt was probably situated somewhere on the east coast of Africa, and the route had not been explored for over 200 years. Punt was known as 'the land of the gods', because myrrh was used as incense in religious ceremonies.

A fleet of vessels was built especially for the trip. No other Egyptian expedition had been planned on such a scale before.

This painted relief† shows gifts being presented to the chief of Punt and his wife.

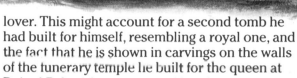

Senmut

A man called Senmut was at Hatshepsut's side throughout her reign. The son of an ordinary official, he became Royal Architect and guardian of the Princess Neferure, as well as holding many other posts. He may also have been Hatshepsut's lover. This might account for a second tomb he had built for himself, resembling a royal one, and the fact that he is shown in carvings on the walls of the funerary temple he built for the queen at Deir el Bahari (reconstructed here).

Hatshepsut's temple at Deir el Bahari was built to a unique design, and much of it has survived.

The temple consisted of a series of huge terraces.

An avenue of sphinxes led up to the first terrace, which was planted with myrrh trees.

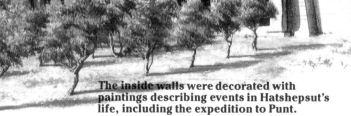

The inside walls were decorated with paintings describing events in Hatshepsut's life, including the expedition to Punt.

Tuthmosis III (1490-1436BC)

Tuthmosis III began his military career in the last years of Hatshepsut's life, and married her second daughter, Meryetre. After Hatshepsut's death, he appears to have ordered the destruction of all her statues and inscriptions. Despite having been kept from power for so long, Tuthmosis was probably the greatest of all the warrior pharaohs. He fought 17 campaigns and enlarged the Egyptian empire to its widest limits.

Tuthmosis III

Key dates

1552-1069BC	New Kingdom	1402-1364BC	Amenhotep III *
1552-1305BC	Dynasty XVIII		
1552-1527BC	Ahmose		
1527-1506BC	Amenhotep I		
1506-1494BC	Tuthmosis I		
1494-1490BC	Tuthmosis II		
1490-1468BC	Hatshepsut		
1490-1436BC	Tuthmosis III		
1438-1412BC	Amenhotep II		
1414-1402BC	Tuthmosis IV		

Amenhotep III hunting

For the remaining kings of Dynasty XVIII, see pages 50-51.

47

The Egyptian army

During the Old and Middle Kingdoms, the Egyptian army consisted of the king's bodyguard and a small army of professional soldiers. Ordinary men could be called up in emergencies, but most lacked military training and so were of limited use. As the *nomarchs*† grew in power they set up armies, which the king sometimes used during a campaign.

This tomb model shows Egyptian soldiers carrying spears and large shields made of wood and leather.

Bows and arrows were the main weapons of Nubian mercenaries, employed from Dynasty VI.

The army in the New Kingdom

The need to drive out the Hyksos (see page 45) and the desire to conquer an empire had brought about a radical reorganization of the army by the New Kingdom. Horses and chariots were introduced and the army increased in size. The king was Commander-in-Chief and often led campaigns himself, while generals and officers of various ranks commanded the units. One out of every 100 able-bodied young men was liable for call-up, but there were usually plenty of volunteers. The army offered adventure and a good career, although not all soldiers went abroad on campaign. Some stayed at home to guard frontiers, suppress civil disturbances or supervise mining and building operations.

The army was made up of several divisions of 5000 men each (4000 foot-soldiers and 1000 charioteers). Charioteers were the elite troops, because of the cost of the equipment and the skill and training involved.

The organization of the army

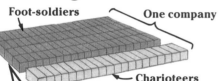

Foot-soldiers
One company
Charioteers

The divisions were named after gods, such as Amun, Ptah, Re and Sutekh (Set). In each one the 4000 foot-soldiers were divided into 20 companies of 200 men each. This diagram shows one division.

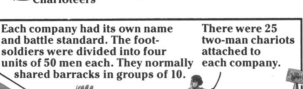

Each company had its own name and battle standard. The foot-soldiers were divided into four units of 50 men each. They normally shared barracks in groups of 10.

One unit

Libyan and Nubian mercenaries formed their own separate units.

Chariots

There were 25 two-man chariots attached to each company.

The battle formation

The first ranks were made up of experienced soldiers.

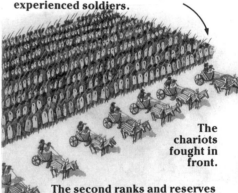

The chariots fought in front.

The second ranks and reserves consisted of the less experienced recruits.

Weapons and training

Egyptian soldiers had to be able to fight with a variety of weapons, including battle axes, maces, spears, swords, daggers and bows and arrows. However, each unit tended to specialize in the use of one particular weapon. Young soldiers were given a rigorous training which included long route marches.

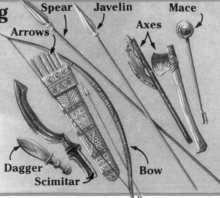

Arrows
Spear
Javelin
Axes
Mace
Dagger
Scimitar
Bow

Weapons were made of bronze and wood.

Armour consisted of bands of leather wrapped around the chest (right). Sometimes metal scales were added (left).

On campaign

Camps were set up when the army was on campaign. The soldiers were accompanied by donkeys carrying baggage and a number of support staff. These included messengers, doctors, priests, armourers and cooks, scouts to spy out the land ahead and grooms to look after the animals. Scribes organized supplies and pay, and kept a daily journal of the campaign.

A defensive mound was dug around the camp.

Shields were placed around the top for added protection.

The tents were laid out in rows. In the centre of the camp were the king's tent and a shrine to Amun.

These golden flies, known as the 'Gold of Valour', were awarded for bravery. Other rewards for a life in the army included the opportunity to take slaves and loot (goods from the enemy), and the prospect of a piece of land on retirement.

Some officers' tents were large enough to have two or more rooms. Pictures show tents equipped with comfortable furniture and provisions. This folding bed belonged to Tutankhamun†.

Sentries

Messenger leaving the camp

Running the empire

The kings of Dynasty XVIII conquered the greatest empire of their day. At its height, it stretched from the Fourth Cataract† of the Nile to northern Syria. The Egyptians acquired great wealth by trading with their subjects and claiming tribute† from them. This is reflected in the amount of treasure buried in tombs during this period.

HITTITES
MITANNIANS
EASTERN EMPIRE
LIBYA
NUBIA
Under Egyptian control
KUSH
Area of Egyptian influence

Nubia

Although the Egyptians met considerable initial opposition in their conquest of Nubia, they managed to maintain peaceful control relatively easily. The Nubians readily adopted many aspects of Egyptian culture, religion, language, writing and architecture.

A Nubian from an Egyptian painting

The Nubian government was run on Egyptian lines, headed by a Viceroy called the 'King's Son of Kush'. He had two deputies; one was responsible for Wawat (northern Nubia), and the other for Kush (southern Nubia). The country was divided into administrative areas, each run by an official who was usually a local chief.

The eastern empire

By contrast, in the eastern part of the empire* the Egyptians encountered cultures almost as old as their own. The area was divided into small princedoms which had well-established traditions of government, law and religion. The Egyptians kept as many native princes as possible in office. Overseers were sent to important cities, but their task was only to guard Egyptian interests. It was the local princes who ruled, through their own officials and according to local laws and customs.

Egyptians storming a Syrian fortress

Trumpet calls were used to sound orders on the battlefield.

As rival empire-builders, the Hittites and the Mitannians were always ready to encourage discontented Egyptian subjects to rebel. To ensure the princes' loyalty and to discourage attacks, Egyptian troops were garrisoned in fortresses and important provincial towns. Rebellions were dealt with severely. However, there were excellent rewards for loyal princes, including opportunities for profitable trade with Egypt. In order to ensure good behaviour, the princes' children were sometimes sent to Egypt as hostages. They were educated at court and treated well. This encouraged them to remain loyal to Egypt when they eventually went home to rule. The pharaohs often reinforced family ties by taking foreign princesses as secondary wives.

*This is the area known as Canaan (see page 25), now occupied by Syria, Lebanon, Israel and Jordan.

The reign of Akhenaten

The reign of Amenhotep IV (1364-1347BC), also known as Akhenaten, still causes great controversies among scholars. Amenhotep is the first person in history who is known to have worshipped only one god. He revived the ancient cult† of the sun god (see page 13), in the form of the Aten (the disc of the sun). Amehotep believed that the Aten revealed himself only to his 'son', the king. He changed his name to Akhenaten ('living spirit of the Aten') in honour of his god.

Akhenaten worshipping the Aten

Akhenaten also gave his wife Nefertiti† (shown here) a second official name incorporating that of the Aten–Neferneferuaten. Normally only kings took a second name.

A painted stone bust of Nefertiti found at Tell el Amarna (see below)

At the start of his reign Akhenaten ordered a complex of shrines to be built for the Aten, beside the temple of Amun-Re at Karnak. However, before it was completed, he decided that the Aten should have a home town of his own. The king sailed north and was inspired by his god to stop at a bay in the cliffs on the east side of the river. There, he ordered a new capital city to be built.

The city of Akhetaten

The king named the new city Akhetaten, meaning 'the Horizon of Aten'. (Its modern name is Tell el Amarna.) The court moved there in the 6th year* of his reign. Excavations have given us a good idea of what the city centre looked like. It had several temples and palaces, as well as luxurious villas for the nobles.

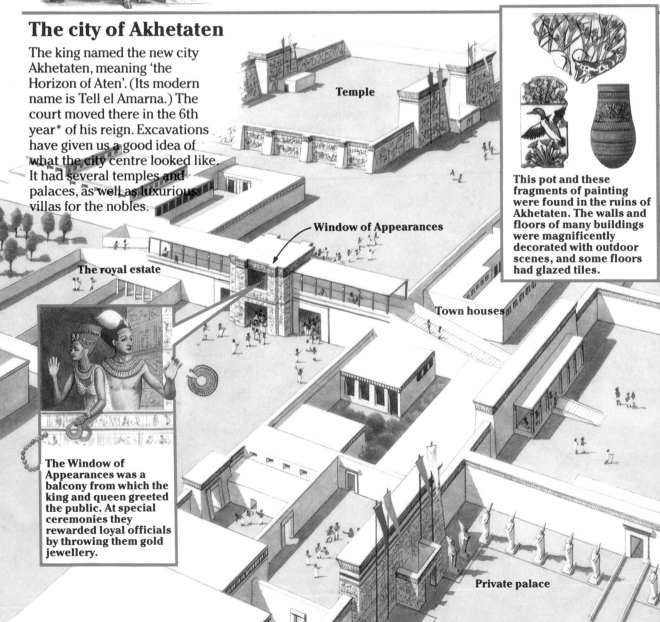

Temple

Window of Appearances

The royal estate

Town houses

This pot and these fragments of painting were found in the ruins of Akhetaten. The walls and floors of many buildings were magnificently decorated with outdoor scenes, and some floors had glazed tiles.

The Window of Appearances was a balcony from which the king and queen greeted the public. At special ceremonies they rewarded loyal officials by throwing them gold jewellery.

Private palace

Akhenaten's religious revolution

Akhenaten introduced a series of changes which amounted to a religious revolution and shocked many conservative Egyptians. Not only did he introduce the worship of the Aten, but at the same time he also banned the worship of all the old Egyptian gods and goddesses. He even had their names cut out of inscriptions.

Experts disagree about Akhenaten's reasons. His actions may have been prompted by devotion to his god, or they may have been the result of a power struggle between the king and the powerful priesthood of Amun-Re.

Offering tables

The Great Temple at Akhetaten was unlike most other New Kingdom temples. It consisted of open courtyards, where the sun's rays could reach the worshippers, with hundreds of tables for offerings.

Portraits of Akhenaten

A carved relief of Akhenaten and his family. The Aten was usually included in portraits.

Akhenaten had himself portrayed in statues and reliefs kissing his wife and playing with his children. The Egyptians were used to more formal traditional portraits and many people must have found these poses rather undignified for a king.

◄ Statue of Akhenaten with feminine hips

Portrait of Akhenaten ► with a long face, and large lips, nose and ears

Some of his ▲ portraits show a more normal looking face.

Kings were traditionally made to look strong, masculine and handsome. However most of Akhenaten's portraits show an almost feminine body, with a long face and large lips, nose and ears. Experts disagree on the reasons for this. If his strange shape was the result of an illness*, it is unlikely that he would have been able to have children. Yet he and Nefertiti had six daughters. So it is possible that portraits were deliberately distorted for some other reason.

The mystery of Smenkhkare

In about year 14 of his reign, Akhenaten took a co-ruler called Smenkhkare, and gave him Nefertiti's special name – Neferneferuaten. Some experts believe he was a young nobleman; others think that he was Akhenaten's brother. However a recent theory suggests that it was Nefertiti herself. According to the theory, Akhenaten believed she would never give birth to a son, so he married their eldest daughter, Meritaten, compensating Nefertiti by making her a 'king'. About the time that Akhenaten died, Smenkhkare also disappeared.

After Akhenaten

Tutankhamun† (1347-1337BC), was probably Akhenaten's son by a minor wife. He became king when he was only about nine and married Ankhesenamun†, the daughter of Akhenaten and Nefertiti. A general called Horemheb† and a courtier called Ay became regents†. They abandoned Akhetaten and restored the worship of the old gods.

Tutankhamun died very young. He was succeeded by Ay and then by Horemheb. It appears from texts written at this period that problems had developed under Akhenaten, including the loss of the northern empire (Syria) to the Hittites†. Horemheb set about reorganizing the government and restoring order. He began a campaign to dishonour Ahkenaten, tearing down many of his monuments. Akhenaten himself was branded as a heretic†.

*The illness referred to is known as Frölich's syndrome.

Egyptian building methods

From the beginning of the Old Kingdom, the Egyptians built enormous stone monuments, such as pyramids and temples. These buildings were constructed without the aid of cranes or other machinery. Instead the work was carried out by large numbers (often thousands) of men, using ropes, ramps and sledges. At first much of the building was done by peasants as a labour tax due to the king. However during the New Kingdom prisoners of war were used as well. All these men had to be housed, fed and looked after. The organization involved was a major feat in itself.

Constructing a temple

When a king wished to build a temple, he summoned his architects, who produced plans, and probably a model, for his approval.

A foundation ceremony was held, during which sacrifices† were made. The king laid out the ground plan with ropes and posts.

Stones were dragged into place to form the bottom layer of the walls. The inside of the building was then filled with sand, forming a flat surface.

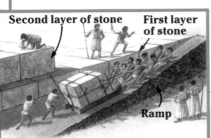

Second layer of stone   First layer of stone

Ramp

A ramp of sand and rubble was built, and the second layer of stone was laid. The interior was filled with sand as before.

Interior filled with rubble and sand

The ramp was raised and lengthened and the process was repeated, layer by layer, until the roof was on. Then the sand and ramps were removed and craftsmen began work on the decoration.

Building a pyramid

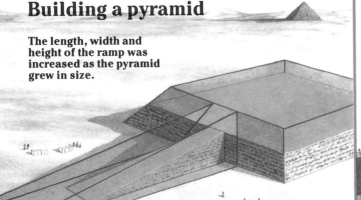

The length, width and height of the ramp was increased as the pyramid grew in size.

Pyramids were also built with ramps, although there are different theories as to how they were arranged. Some experts believe that only one ramp was used. Others suggest that ramps were built on each side of the pyramid.

Raising an obelisk

Ramps were also used for raising obelisks (monuments to the sun god).

First a stone base was constructed, surrounded by a brick funnel and long ramps. The funnel was filled with sand.

Hundreds of men were used to haul the obelisk up the ramp, base first. It was carefully manoeuvred on to the mouth of the funnel.

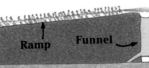

Obelisk

Ramp   Funnel   Base

A hole was made here to remove the sand.

As the sand level sank, the men guided the obelisk so that it tilted up, slid down and rested on its base. The ramps and funnel were then dismantled.

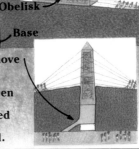

Architectural details

Egyptian craftsmen reproduced in stone many of the features of the earlier reed buildings (see page 9).

Stone pillars were carved to look like bunches of reeds and flowers.

The tops of walls were often decorated with a *kheker* frieze, which represented reeds bound together.

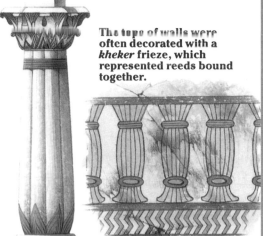

Statues

Statues were shaped with stone pounders. Copper and bronze tools and abrasive powders were used to cut and polish the stone, and to carve details such as plaits in wigs. Some statues were colossal.

Paintings

Tombs and temples were brightly decorated, inside and out, by skilled artists. The paintings had an important religious and magical purpose. The Egyptians believed that the gods, or the dead person, could actually take part in the activities shown in the picture. For example, a painting of a banquet would ensure that the dead person ate well in the Next World†.

Carving reliefs

A raised relief (a sculpture carved on a background) was made by cutting away the background and modelling details on to the figures.

Raised relief

Sunken relief

A sunken relief was made by cutting away the stone from inside the outline of the figure and carving the details out of the body.

Before painting a wall, the artist made sure the surface was flat, usually by applying a layer of plaster. A grid was then printed on the wall, using string soaked in red paint.

The artist drew in the outlines in red. These were corrected in black by a supervisor. Then the background colour was filled in, followed by the figures, and finally details such as eyes.

Face in profile

Eye looks straight ahead

Shoulders from the front

Breast in profile

Navel in ¾ twist

Legs in profile

Egyptian painting was governed by strict rules of proportion. The figures were painted as if seen from different angles at once. Some parts were shown from the front, while others were in profile.

The paints were made from chalks, ochres (earth) and minerals such as copper and cobalt. These were ground into powder and mixed with water. The brushes were made of reeds.

Egyptian houses

The Egyptians lacked good timber but had plenty of mud and reeds, so the earliest houses were made from reeds, woven and bound together. By the Gerzean Period (see page 9), most houses were built from bricks made of sun-dried mud, and reeds were only used for temporary shelters. The reconstruction below shows a rich nobleman's house from the New Kingdom. By this time most houses, from farmhouses to luxurious villas, were divided into three main areas. There was a reception at the front where business was done, a hall in the centre where friends were entertained, and private quarters at the back where the family lived.

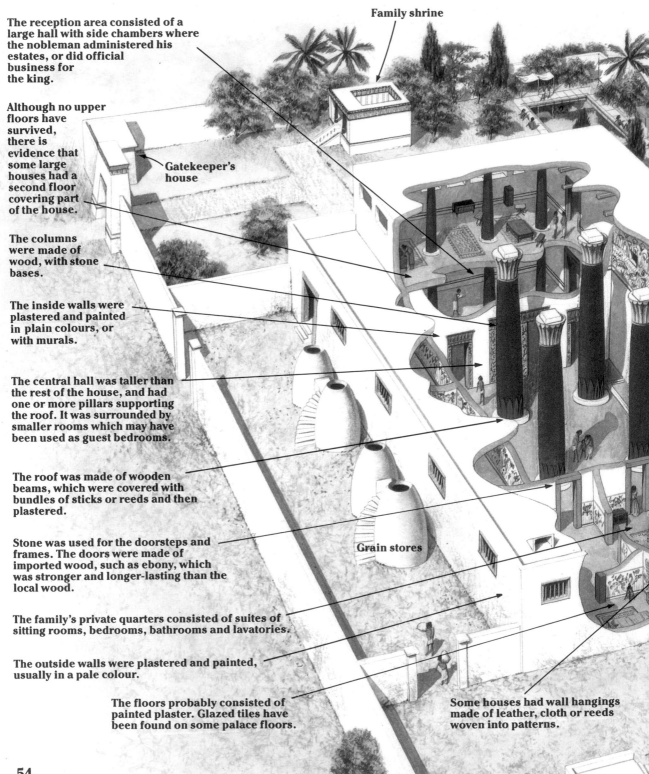

Family shrine

The reception area consisted of a large hall with side chambers where the nobleman administered his estates, or did official business for the king.

Although no upper floors have survived, there is evidence that some large houses had a second floor covering part of the house.

Gatekeeper's house

The columns were made of wood, with stone bases.

The inside walls were plastered and painted in plain colours, or with murals.

The central hall was taller than the rest of the house, and had one or more pillars supporting the roof. It was surrounded by smaller rooms which may have been used as guest bedrooms.

The roof was made of wooden beams, which were covered with bundles of sticks or reeds and then plastered.

Stone was used for the doorsteps and frames. The doors were made of imported wood, such as ebony, which was stronger and longer-lasting than the local wood.

Grain stores

The family's private quarters consisted of suites of sitting rooms, bedrooms, bathrooms and lavatories.

The outside walls were plastered and painted, usually in a pale colour.

The floors probably consisted of painted plaster. Glazed tiles have been found on some palace floors.

Some houses had wall hangings made of leather, cloth or reeds woven into patterns.

How we know what houses looked like

During the First Intermediate Period and the Middle Kingdom, pottery models of houses were placed in tombs. The model below has been used to reconstruct the Middle Kingdom farmhouse shown on the right.

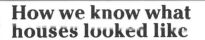

A Middle Kingdom farmhouse

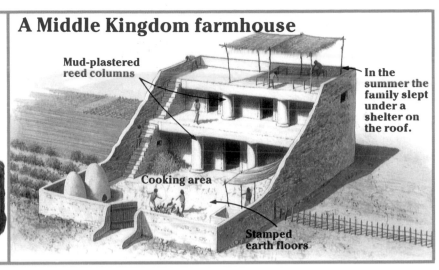

Mud-plastered reed columns

In the summer the family slept under a shelter on the roof.

Cooking area

Stamped earth floors

The Egyptians loved gardens and pools, but very few people would have been able to afford a garden like this one.

Plastered mud-brick stairs led to the roof and the upper floors.

In summer people may have slept on the roof. Some houses even had rooms on the roof, which were open on one side.

Well

Cattle pens

Bedrooms

Windows were at ceiling level. The frames and sills were made of mud, wood or stone, and some had grills in them. There was no glass.

Tomb paintings show some houses with vents on the roof. This enabled air to reach the rooms below.

Mats were often hung over windows and open doors, to keep out flies, dust and hot sunlight.

Wine press

Kitchen

Stables

Servants' quarters

Furniture

The furniture of kings and nobles has been preserved in tombs. It was made of imported woods, such as ebony and cedar, inlaid with ivory, precious metals, semi-precious stones and faience†. Most furniture was probably made of cheap local wood, leather or reeds, and might have been painted.

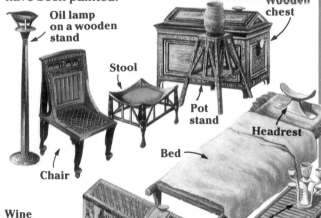

Oil lamp on a wooden stand

Wooden chest

Stool

Pot stand

Headrest

Bed

Chair

Chest

Oil lamp made of alabaster†

Game board

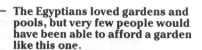

Town houses

Very few Egyptian towns have been excavated, as people have continued living in them over the centuries, and modern towns have been built on top of the ancient sites. However, models and paintings suggest that some houses were up to four storeys high. Towns were hot, noisy, dusty places, with narrow, busy streets. Water was supplied from private and public wells, but there does not appear to have been a public refuse or sewage system. Each household had to dispose of its own waste – in pits, in the river, or in the streets.

The family quarters were on the upper floors.

Shops and businesses were probably on the ground floor.

People spent a lot of time on the roof because it was cooler. In the summer they probably slept there too.

Cooking and eating

The Egyptians cooked in the open air whenever possible, to avoid the danger of fire. However, evidence from Tell el Amarna (see page 50) shows that some people risked cooking on the roof. Egyptian food was baked, boiled, stewed, fried, grilled or roasted.

Cooking was done on tripods (shown here), braziers or pottery stoves.

Wood was used as fuel. It was set alight with a firedrill, which created heat by means of friction.

Tripod

Paintings like this one, as well as offerings and models left in tombs, give us an idea of what the Egyptians ate and how it was prepared. Although no recipes have been found, there are references in texts to soups and sauces.

Pots and pans

Kitchen equipment found in tombs, includes pots, pans, storage jars, ladles, sieves and whisks.

Storage jars

Whisk

Sieve

Bowl

Drinking cup

Beer jar with straw

Most dishes were made of earthenware, although rich people also used faience†, bronze, silver and gold.

Dish

Bread, beer and wine

Bread and beer were the staple elements of the Egyptian diet. To make bread, the wheat was first ground into flour. Evidence is recorded of requests for pure wheat flour, sieved and free from added barley, so some people must have cheated by mixing barley with the wheat. The flour was then mixed with water to form a dough. Bread was baked in moulds inside the oven, or shaped into flat, round loaves, which were placed on the outside of it. As the flour was ground outdoors, grit often got into the bread, causing heavy wear on people's teeth.

Women ground the wheat into flour. If very fine flour was needed, it was then pounded by men.

Flavourings were sometimes added to the dough, such as honey, fruit, butter, seeds or herbs.

Bread moulds

Oven

The loaves dropped off the oven when they were cooked.

Making wine

Although the Egyptians made several types of wine, it was usually only drunk by the rich. Wine was made from dates, pomegranates and palm sap, as well as from grapes. The best vineyards were said to be in the Nile Delta.

Trellises for growing grapes

To extract the juice, men ▶ trod on the grapes in a large vat. This produced the best quality wine.

Then the fruit pulp, pips and stalks were all crushed together in a sack, twisted between two poles. This produced more juice, but it made a poorer quality wine.

◀ The juice was put in jars to ferment. The mouths of the jars were closed with a wad of leaves plastered over with mud.

Small holes were left in the stoppers, to allow further fermentation to take place without the jars exploding.

Finally the jars were completely sealed. They were labelled with details of the year, the vineyard and the quality of the wine.

Making beer

To make beer, barley was moistened with water and left to stand. Lightly baked barley loaves were then broken up and mixed with the grain in a large jar of water. The mixture then fermented (turned into alcohol).

The mixture was thick and lumpy.

Breaking bread into the mixture

Beer was strained through a sieve before being served.

Beer was served in a drinking cup. It was sometimes drunk through a straw, made from wood or metal.

Women and family life

In many ways, women in Egypt were in a more privileged position than elsewhere in the Ancient World. Although they did not hold jobs in government, they had a great deal of personal freedom and had the same legal rights and obligations as men. They were able to do business deals, enter into contracts and act as witnesses in court, and they were expected to conduct their own court cases. Women took the same oaths as men and faced the same penalties.

Children

The Egyptians regarded children as a great blessing. If a couple had no children, they prayed to gods and goddesses for help, or placed letters in the tombs of dead relatives, asking them to use their influence with the gods. Some people also tried fertility charms and magic. If all this failed, children could be adopted.

From an early age boys were taught their fathers' trades and girls worked with their mothers at home. People who could afford it sent their sons to school from the age of about seven (see page 64). Although there is no evidence of any schools for girls, some learned to read and write at home, and a few even became doctors.

Wills and inheritance

Children were expected to look after their elderly parents, and to organize funerals. At one time the person who paid for the funeral also inherited the property.

Fathers tended to leave land to their sons, and other property, such as the house, furniture and jewellery, to the daughters. However there was nothing to prevent girls from inheriting estates, especially if they had no brothers. There is evidence of Middle Kingdom heiresses who inherited whole *nomes*†.

New Kingdom land-owner supervising her estate

Jobs and careers

Although women usually married young and were expected to play a major part in bringing up their children, there were a few jobs and careers open to them.

Courts and temples employed women as singers, dancers, musicians and acrobats. Noblewomen could become courtiers or priestesses.

Acrobat

Professional mourner

Priestess

Women also worked as perfume-makers (shown below), gardeners, weavers and professional mourners.

There is evidence of women running farms and businesses on behalf of absent husbands and sons. This scene shows a woman supervising farm workers.

Statuette of servant girl

◀ Some women worked as servants in wealthy households. A noblewoman's maid or nanny could have great influence. The sons of some royal nannies held important positions at court.

Marriage

Peasant girls sometimes married as early as 12 years old; those from richer families were a few years older. The boys were usually a few years older than the girls. Parents were expected to choose their children's husbands and wives for them, although surviving love poetry suggests that some young people chose their own.

Statue of a New Kingdom couple

Details of the marriage ceremony are not known, but it probably began with a procession, followed by an exchange of vows by the bride and groom, a banquet and the giving of presents. Most couples moved into a house of their own, usually provided by the husband. Egyptian texts warn about the many problems that arise from living with parents and in-laws.

The marriage contract contained detailed financial arrangements. The wife was entitled to a maintenance allowance from her husband. She brought goods with her, such as clothes and furniture, as a kind of dowry†. But, unlike a dowry, the goods remained hers. They, or others of equivalent value, had to be returned to her if the marriage ended for any reason.

Both husband and wife could own property of their own, separate from their partners. For practical reasons, it was usual for a wife to let her husband administer her property along with his, but it was still regarded as hers.

The marriage fund

From the Middle Kingdom onwards, a joint marriage fund was set up and a written record was kept. The husband contributed two-thirds and the wife one-third; these proportions remained the same, even if the value of the fund increased over the years. The fund acted as a guaranteed inheritance for the children. When a husband or wife died, his or her share went straight to the children. If the surviving partner remarried, the children received the rest of the inheritance before a new fund was set up for the second marriage. If a couple divorced, they would each keep their own share of the fund, although the wife forfeited hers if she had been unfaithful to her husband. Some unscrupulous men accused their wives falsely, in order to confiscate their share, but the woman was allowed to keep it if she took an oath that she was innocent.

Divorce

A wife was known as the *nebet per* (lady of house). She was in charge of running the house and bringing up the children, and expected to be treated with respect. If a wife was treated badly, she usually went to her relatives for help. They might try to persuade the husband to improve his behaviour, making him swear to do so in front of them. Divorce appears to have been an easy matter, amounting to a simple statement before witnesses. A divorced woman usually had custody of her children and was free to remarry.

Concubines

Royal harem

Although kings always had several wives, an ordinary Egyptian man normally only had one. However, it was considered legal and respectable for a man to keep an official lover (known as a concubine), if he could afford one. Although the man's wife and children came first, he was also expected to look after the concubine and her children.

The king's wives and concubines all lived together in a special part of the palace. Unlike some later harems†, which were cut off from the world, this was a lively, open place, where officials and other visitors could be received.

Egyptian temples

For the Egyptians a temple was the home on earth of the god or goddess to whom it was dedicated. It housed a cult statue, a statue of the deity through which the spirit of the god or goddess was said to communicate. A temple was not like a church, mosque or synagogue, where people gather together to worship. It was a private place. Normally only priests and priestesses went inside. Most ordinary people only went as far as the entrance to make offerings and pray. At some festivals, the cult statue was carried out of the temple in a boat, called a sacred barque.

This is a New Kingdom temple. It was built inside an enclosure which contained several outbuildings, and was entered through a gateway called a *pylon*. The temple itself was divided into three areas – the courtyards (one or more), the hypostyle hall, and the sanctuary.

Priests and priestesses

Each temple had a number of priests and priestesses. The priests were divided into four groups, called *phyles*. Each *phyle* went on duty three times a year, for a month at a time. The temple also provided work for other people, including scribes, singers, musicians, craftsmen, builders and farmers.

At one time if a person wanted the god's help he or she placed a small *stela*† of a pair of ears against the temple wall. This was to remind the god to listen to the person's prayers.

Temple workshops produced goods such as furniture, statues, linen and sacred vessels.

Flagpoles

Obelisks (sacred monuments to the sun god)

Pylon

Sphinxes were carved figures with a lion's body and a ram's head. They represented the sun god.

Avenue of sphinxes†

Some people prayed before statues of the king. The Egyptians believed he was descended from the gods and could intercede with them on behalf of his subjects.

Scribes† sat at the temple gates. If someone wanted to ask the god a question, they asked the scribe to write it down. The question was then given to the priests in the temple.

The outer walls of the temple were decorated with inscriptions and scenes of the king's conquests.

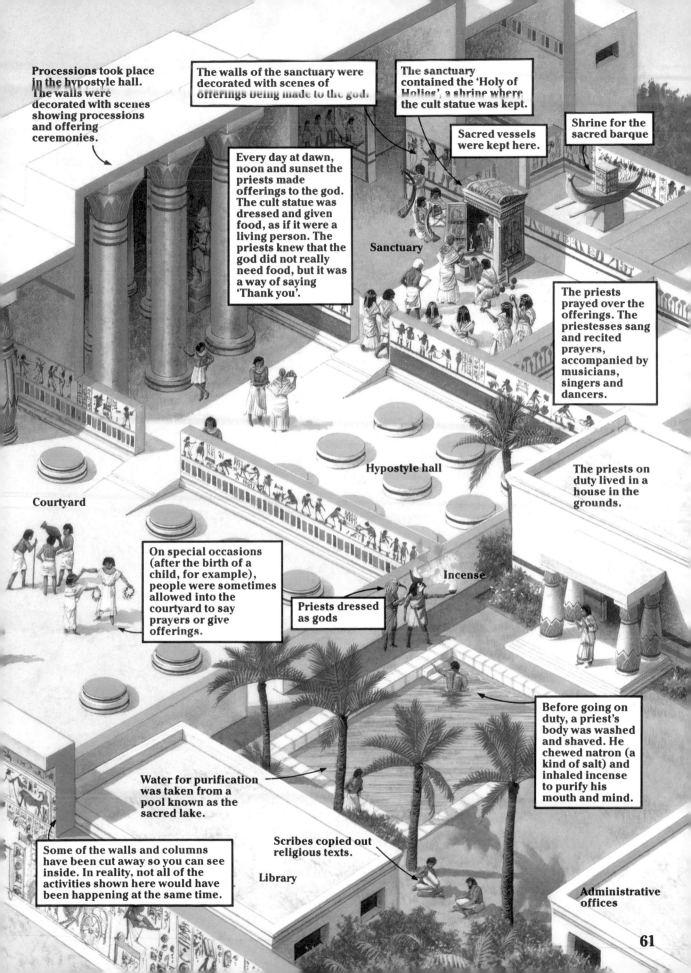

Processions took place in the hypostyle hall. The walls were decorated with scenes showing processions and offering ceremonies.

The walls of the sanctuary were decorated with scenes of offerings being made to the god.

The sanctuary contained the 'Holy of Holies', a shrine where the cult statue was kept.

Shrine for the sacred barque

Sacred vessels were kept here.

Every day at dawn, noon and sunset the priests made offerings to the god. The cult statue was dressed and given food, as if it were a living person. The priests knew that the god did not really need food, but it was a way of saying 'Thank you'.

Sanctuary

The priests prayed over the offerings. The priestesses sang and recited prayers, accompanied by musicians, singers and dancers.

Hypostyle hall

The priests on duty lived in a house in the grounds.

Courtyard

On special occasions (after the birth of a child, for example), people were sometimes allowed into the courtyard to say prayers or give offerings.

Priests dressed as gods

Incense

Before going on duty, a priest's body was washed and shaved. He chewed natron (a kind of salt) and inhaled incense to purify his mouth and mind.

Water for purification was taken from a pool known as the sacred lake.

Scribes copied out religious texts.

Some of the walls and columns have been cut away so you can see inside. In reality, not all of the activities shown here would have been happening at the same time.

Library

Administrative offices

Dreams and oracles

Like many other ancient peoples, the Egyptians tried various methods to interpret the will of the gods and to predict the future. One of these was through dreams. It was usual for a pharaoh to claim that a god had appeared to him in a dream, to order him to pursue a particular policy, reassure him of support or warn him of danger.

People who were puzzled by dreams could consult priests. They were trained to interpret dreams and had books to help them. Here are two examples adapted from Egyptian texts.

If a person dreamed about looking at a large cat, it meant that there would be a large harvest.

If a man dreamed about looking at his face in a mirror, it meant he would have another wife.

Signs in the sky

People also looked for meanings in the sky. When Tuthmosis III† saw a falling star, he believed it was sent to reassure him of victory in battle.

Consulting the oracle

The most popular method of finding out the will of the gods was to consult the oracle. This was usually a cult statue†, through which the god was supposed to speak. Kings sometimes used the oracle to gain approval for royal policy, and ordinary people sought solutions to personal problems and fears.

The oracle was normally consulted on a feast day. The cult statue was carried out of the temple on its sacred barque†. Anyone could approach and ask a question. The answer (yes or no) depended on how the boat moved – forwards or backwards, or pressing down. Obviously the result of an oracle could be fixed, but most priests probably believed that the gods inspired their responses.

Mesopotamia

The people of Mesopotamia had a variety of ways of predicting the future and finding out the will of the gods. They looked carefully at the behaviour of animals. They also sought information from arrows thrown in the ground, shapes made by smoke or oil poured on water, and from the entrails of sacrificed animals. The Babylonians specialized in reading omens (signs of some future event) from animal livers.

Hiring a scribe

Between festivals, anyone who wanted to ask a question urgently could go to the temple gate. As most people could not read or write, they hired a scribe† to write their questions down. The questions were then given to a priest, who consulted the god on the people's behalf.

Sacred animals

Many Egyptian gods and goddesses were associated with a particular species of animal or bird (see pages 20-21). It became the custom for a creature of that species to be selected and kept in the deity's main temple. The animal was treated with great honour, and people believed that when certain prayers and spells had been said, the spirit of the deity passed into it. The animal could then give oracles, indicating a yes or no answer by its movements.

These are examples of sacred animals that were kept at temples. The deity's name is in brackets.

Hawk at Edfu (Horus)

Cat at Bubastis (Bast)

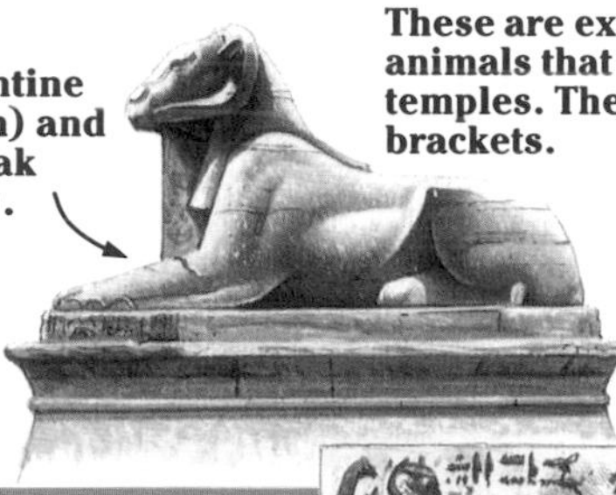

Ram at Elephantine (Khnum) and at Karnak (Amun).

Crocodile at Medinet el Fayum and Kom-ombo (Sobek)

The Apis bull

Relief† showing Apis bull ▶

The animal we know most about was the Apis bull. He was associated with the god Ptah, whose cult temple† was at Memphis. Whenever an Apis bull died, a search was made all over Egypt for his successor. The new bull had to be black and white with certain special features – a white triangular patch on his forehead, a patch resembling a flying vulture on his back, a scarab-shaped lump on his tongue, and double hairs in his tail.

Once the Apis had been identified, he and his mother were taken to Memphis, where they lived in comfort for the rest of their lives. Their dung and milk were used for magic and medicinal purposes.

Funeral procession of Apis bull

At great religious festivals, the spirit of Ptah was believed to enter the bull and he was paraded before the people so that they could worship the god through him. When the bull died, he became known as the Osiris-Apis. He was embalmed and taken in a great procession to the Serapeum (the tomb of the bulls) at Sakkara. There he was buried in a huge *sarcophagus* (a stone coffin).

Animal mummies

Mummified cat

By the Late Period, some entire species of animals were regarded as almost sacred. It then became the custom to give these animals proper burials. People believed that by doing this they would please the gods. Many animal cemeteries have been found. The largest seems to have been at Sakkara, where there are enormous underground passages. Millions of birds (such as ibises and hawks), cats, dogs, baboons and other animals have been found there.

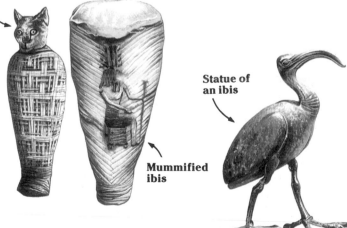

Statue of an ibis

Mummified ibis

Education

During the Old Kingdom the sons of noblemen were educated at home. When they became young men, they were instructed in intellectual, social and spiritual arts by older men with a reputation for being wise.

The first evidence of schools in Egypt dates from the Middle Kingdom, although they may have developed earlier. Many schools were attached to temples; the best ones were probably at large temples, like Memphis and Thebes. There were village schools too, where a few peasant boys were taught by a local priest or scribe who wanted to supplement his income. However, most Egyptian children did not go to school. Instead most boys learned their fathers' trade, while girls helped their mothers at home.

A temple school

Temple schools were probably connected to the 'House of Life', a complex of buildings where religious texts were copied and stored.

Egyptian schools were for boys only. The boys began when they were about seven years old. They learned to read and write the three forms of Egyptian script (see page 11). Most of their time was spent copying texts.

The boys wrote on pieces of broken pottery or stone, known as *ostraca* (sing: *ostracon*), or on wooden tablets covered with plaster, which could be washed and re-used.

This is an *ostracon* with part of the *Story of Sinuhe*, a popular Egyptian tale

Higher education

At the age of nine or ten, a boy could go on to higher education. At this stage he learned how to compose letters and legal documents, and studied a range of subjects, including history, literature, geography, religion, languages, surveying, engineering, account-keeping, astronomy, maths and medicine. Evidence

Papyrus with mathematical text

suggests that examinations were held, but we do not know at what stage they were taken.

Those who could afford it went on to specialize in one or two subjects. A poor boy's family might try to persuade a rich man to be his patron†, in order to pay for his studies. Most well-educated boys eventually became scribes†. This was the most highly regarded profession in Egypt, as most people could not read and write and the whole system of government was based on keeping records. Some scribes entered government service and became important officials.

Sumerian education and learning

The Sumerians were expert mathematicians, astronomers and surveyors. They also developed elaborate law codes. Their calendar, based on the Moon, had months of 28 days. The Sumerians used two counting systems. One was a decimal system like ours, based on a unit of ten. The other, based on units of sixty, is still used for measuring circles and time. The Sumerians were the first to divide an hour into 60 minutes and a circle into 360°.

Sumerian tablet with mathematical text

A Sumerian school

Wealthy Sumerians sent their sons to schools, where they learned reading, writing and arithmetic. The boys practised writing on soft clay tablets, which could be squashed, reshaped and used again. The school day was long and discipline was strict. Boys were beaten for not learning their lessons properly.

Stars, calendars and measuring systems

The Egyptians were very interested in astronomy. They understood that there were differences between planets and stars and were able to identify Mercury, Mars, Venus, Jupiter and Saturn. They used their knowledge of the stars to work out several calendars.

Egyptian calendars

This Egyptian astronomical drawing shows the constellations (groups of stars) as gods.

The first Egyptian calendar was based on the stars. The most important star was Sirius, which the Egyptians called Sopdet (or Sothis, its Greek name). The Egyptians noticed that Sopdet disappeared below the horizon at the same time each year, and reappeared just before sunrise 70 days later. This happened just when the level of the Nile began to rise for the annual floods. It became the date of their New Year, which was called *wepet renpet*.

Their second calendar was based on the cycle of the Moon. As a lunar month consists of 29½ days, the calendar was in constant need of adjustment. However, it continued to be used to calculate the dates of some religious festivals.

The first calendar to divide the year into 365 days was introduced very early in the Old Kingdom, possibly by Imhotep†. Since there are actually 365¼ days in a year, this calendar slipped very gradually out of step with the New Year as calculated by Sopdet. When Julius Caesar† visited Egypt, he was so impressed by the calendar that he took it back to Rome and adapted it. His version, known as the Julian calendar, was used until the Gregorian calendar (the one we use today) was introduced in the 16th century.

The Egyptian year

10 DAYS = ONE WEEK

3 WEEKS = ONE MONTH (30 days)

4 MONTHS = ONE SEASON (120 days)

3 SEASONS = 360 DAYS

+ 5 HOLY DAYS

= ONE YEAR (365 days)

Holy days

The five holy days were the birthdays of Osiris, Isis, Set, Nephthys and Horus, which all came at the end of the year. These, and other important festivals, were public holidays. Every tenth day was also a holiday, rather like a weekend.

Osiris   Isis

Days

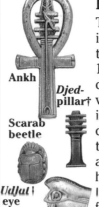

Ankh

Djed-pillar†

Scarab beetle

Udjat† eye

The Egyptians were the first to introduce the 24 hour day, which they divided into 12 hours of day and 12 of night. They believed that some days were good, while others were very unlucky. (This related to events in the lives of the gods.) On a bad day, it was considered advisable to take extra care and wear plenty of amulets (magic charms, shown here). On the worst days it was best to stay at home and pray, and wait for the danger to pass.

Dates

The Egyptians counted their years from the accession of the reigning king. So when a new king came to the throne, they began again at year 1. Since scholars know who reigned, in what order, and for how long, they can add up the reign dates and convert them into dates BC.

Telling the time

Spout

An Egyptian water clock

The Egyptians told the time by means of a water clock, a conical vessel with hours marked off on the inside. Water dripped out of a spout at the bottom at a carefully measured rate. As the water level fell, the number of marks that were exposed indicated the time.

Egyptian measurements

Egyptian measurements were based on the human body. The main measurement was called a *cubit* and was equal to the distance from the elbow to the fingertip. Seven hands, each four fingers wide, also equalled one *cubit*. A *cubit* was then divided into digits (finger-widths), and then sub-divided into fractions of a digit.

An Egyptian measuring rod

Crafts and trades

The craftsmen and women of Egypt were well-paid and respected members of the community. The most highly skilled were employed in temple and palace workshops or on the estates of nobles. There were also village craftsmen who produced goods for the local market and probably did a little farming to supplement their income.

A boy usually followed his family's trade, although he could be trained in another craft if he showed a special talent for it. After training as an apprentice, he was promoted to 'junior', and then craftsman. If he was very skilled, he became a master craftsman. There were a few trades open to women, including weaving, gardening and making perfume.

Experts have been able to learn a lot about the techniques of Egyptian craftsmen from paintings and models left in tombs, as well as from the objects they made. This painting shows goldsmiths at work.

The royal tomb-builders

Excavations at Deir el Medinah on the West Bank near Thebes have uncovered a village designed specially for the men who built the royal tombs of the New Kingdom. The village was abandoned at the end of this period, when the kings were no longer buried at Thebes.

Excavations have revealed the layout of the village. Surviving texts on *ostraca*† provide information about the lives of skilled workmen in Egypt, although as royal tomb-builders these men were probably unusually privileged. There were 60 qualified workmen, as well as juniors and apprentices. They were divided into two teams, each under the direction of a foreman and his deputy. The week was ten days long and included two days' holiday. There were also holidays for religious festivals. The working day was in two shifts, each four hours long, with a rest at midday. This reconstruction shows what the village might have looked like.

The village was surrounded by a wall. The main street was straight and narrow, and lined with small houses, mostly identical in design.

During the week the men lived in barracks in the Valley of the Kings, returning to the village for weekends and holidays.

Wages were paid in goods – food, drink, linen, oil, fuel and salt, with bonuses of silver on special occasions. The foremen were paid twice as much as ordinary workmen.

A doctor and two scribes† were attached to the village. The scribes kept records of work, tools and wages, and wrote down the villagers' questions to the oracle†.

The king provided 15 female slaves to grind grain for the villagers. Male servants carried water, cut firewood and washed clothes.

Tools and techniques

Here is a selection of different Egyptian crafts, showing some of the tools and techniques that were used.

Most cutting tools were made from flint and obsidian.

A bow-drill was used to drill holes in beads and inside stone vases.

Stone vase

Carpentry

This carpenter's workshop has been reconstructed from a painting.

Polishing wood with sandstone

Sawing

Cutting wood with a saw

Making a hollow with a mallet and chisel

Some carpenters' tools have survived in tombs. They were made of copper and bronze, and had wooden handles.

Metalworking

Egyptian metalsmiths worked in copper, bronze, silver, gold and electrum. This scene shows copper being smelted (extracted from the ore). Using bellows to keep the fire blazing fiercely, the ore was heated until it melted. The molten metal was then poured into a mould to shape it.

Bellows

Molten copper

Mould

Lost-wax casting

A technique called lost-wax casting was used to shape finer objects such as ornaments. This process is still in use.

The statue was modelled in wax around a clay core, then covered in clay to form the mould. Pegs kept the clay in place.

The clay was then heated and the wax melted.

The wax was poured away and the empty space was filled with molten metal. When it cooled, the clay was broken, exposing the statue.

Pottery

Pots were shaped on a potter's wheel. The pots were then fired (baked) in a wood-burning kiln. The fire had to be tended carefully to stop the temperature from dropping.

Kiln

Wheel

Paper-making

The Egyptians wrote on a paper called papyrus made from papyrus reeds. Strips of pith from inside the reed were laid flat. Another layer was laid across them, at right angles. This was pounded and pressed under heavy weights, until the paper was welded together.

Papyrus

Strips of pith

Boat-building

Lightweight ▶ papyrus boats were made by tying bundles of reeds together.

To build a wooden boat, planks were lashed and pegged together with ▼ dowels.

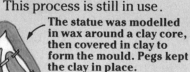

Glass-making

Glass containers were made by dipping a sandy clay core into a dish of molten glass. Patterns were made by winding glass threads around the core, and then heating and flattening them.

Egyptian glass vase

Weaving

The first Egyptian looms were laid out horizontally on the ground, and held in place with pegs. ▼

From about 1500BC vertical looms were in use. These were more practical to use indoors as they took up less space.

Leather working

Leatherworkers made a range of things, including sandals, shields, armour, arrow quivers and furniture.

The Amarna letters

In 1887 an Egyptian peasant woman, digging for mud-bricks in the ruins of the city of Amarna (see page 50), discovered several hundred baked clay tablets. They turned out to be government records from Akhenaten's† reign, consisting of letters written to the pharaoh by a number of foreign kings and princes. Although many of the tablets were damaged or destroyed before they reached the experts, the ones that survived have given historians a vivid picture of the Egyptian world in about 1350BC. The tablets (which are known as the Amarna letters) provide interesting information about the politics and diplomacy of the time.

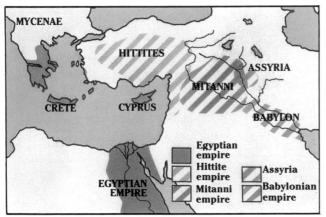

At the start of Akhenaten's reign there were four great empires – those of Egypt, Mitanni, Babylon and the Hittites. Other major powers included Assyria, Cyprus and Mycenae.

Great importance was attached to the way rulers addressed one another. 'Brother' was only used by equals, 'father' by an independent ruler to a friendly but more powerful one, and 'lord' by a subject prince to his conqueror. We know that the King of Babylon was furious when he discovered that his former subject, the King of Assyria, had addressed the pharaoh as 'brother'.

The pharaoh

Assyrian messenger reading a letter

Ambassadors, equipped with letters of introduction and requests for safe conduct, travelled far afield to negotiate on behalf of their rulers. Messengers maintained a courier service, carrying royal correspondence in sealed pouches around their necks.

Mitanni bride

Marriages were a useful way of cementing alliances. Tuthmosis IV married a Mitannian princess as part of a peace settlement. His son and grandson also married Mitannian princesses. Egyptian princesses, on the other hand, never married foreigners, presumably to prevent a foreigner from having a claim to the Egyptian throne. When a Babylonian king asked for an Egyptian bride, he was firmly refused.

There were regular exchanges of gifts between kings, sometimes as a result of specific requests. In one letter, a Hittite king asked his 'brother' in Babylon to send him young stallions (because old ones would not survive the winters). A Mitanni king asked for gold, claiming that 'in my brother's land [Egypt] gold is as the dust'. There were complaints if a messenger arrived without a gift or if the quality of a gift was inferior.

These Babylonians are presenting horses to the Hittite king.

Diplomatic etiquette was important. It was considered necessary to exchange letters of congratulation or condolence where appropriate. On one occasion, the King of Babylon complained bitterly when he received no letters or presents from Queen Meritaten of Egypt during an illness.

However all this politeness concealed grim struggles for power. It appears that many Egyptian subject princes wrote to the pharaoh accusing rival princes of disloyalty, in the hope of taking over their land. One of them, the ambitious Prince of Amurru, attacked the cities of fellow Egyptian vassals†, claiming that they were disloyal to Egypt. One of his victims, Prince Rib-addi of Byblos, begged for Akhenaten's help, but his pleas were ignored. This attitude cost Akhenaten the northern provinces of his empire. The Prince of Amurru, having conquered several cities, defected to the Hittites, joined by other princes who believed that the pharaoh would be as indifferent to them as he had been to Rib-addi.

Ramesses the Great and Dynasty XIX

Horemheb†, the last king of Dynasty XVIII (see page 51), died without a son. The throne passed to his Vizier, a former army officer called Ramesses. He became Ramesses I and founded a new dynasty, Dynasty XIX. The new king was already an old man, and was soon succeeded by his son Seti (named after the god Set, one of the patron gods of his family).

Seti I

Seti I
(1303-1289BC)

Seti I had the task of preserving the remains of Egypt's eastern empire from the expansion of the Hittites†. He fought several long and successful campaigns, but each time he returned home the Hittites took the opportunity to reoccupy and seize some Egyptian territory.

Seti restored some of the monuments damaged during Akhenaten's reign (see pages 50-51) and built new temples to the old gods.

In order to strengthen the new dynasty, Seti had his son Ramesses crowned during his own lifetime. He also provided him with a harem†, with the result that when Seti died, Ramesses II succeeded peacefully to the throne, having already fathered several children.

Ramesses II

Ramesses II reigned for 67 years and lived to be over 90. He was a great warrior (see page 70) and a prolific builder, commissioning temples throughout Egypt and Nubia. He was also an excellent self-publicist. Amongst other things, he claimed that the god Amun was his real father.

Ramesses II (1289-1224BC)

This is a reconstruction of the hypostyle hall of the Temple of Amun at Karnak, built by Ramesses II.

The most spectacular of Ramesses' temples were the two that were cut into the rock face at Abu Simbel in Nubia, one of which is reconstructed here.

Ramesses' other buildings included fortresses to protect the western frontier from the Libyans, and a city and palace, known as the House of Ramesses, which was built near the site of the old Hyksos† capital at Avaris. He also had his name engraved on some of the buildings and statues of previous kings, making it look as if he had built them as well.

Later generations of Egyptians saw him as one of the most successful kings in their history, although this judgement owes a certain amount to the power of propaganda.

◄ This painted relief† shows Ramesses II overpowering his enemies. The three prisoners shown are a Libyan, a Syrian and a Nubian.

Ramesses had many wives and concubines† who between them had about 200 children. He built the second temple at Abu Simbel for his chief queen, Nefertari†, as well as a tomb in the Valley of the Queens near Thebes. When Nefertari died, Ramesses married their daughter Meryet-Amun, and another wife, Isi-nofret, became chief queen. His other wives included his daughter Bint-Anath†, one of his sisters, and a Hittite princess.

This wall-painting from Nefertari's tomb shows the Queen playing a board game.

The struggle with the Hittites

In the first half of his reign Ramesses was engaged in a bitter struggle with the expanding empire of the Hittites†. After some successful campaigning, he set out in year 5* to capture the city of Kadesh, an ally of the Hittites.

Ramesses was tricked by two bedouin† who were secretly working for the Hittites. He approached Kadesh, accompanied only by his bodyguard and the division of Amun**. The bedouin had claimed that the Hittite army was about 200km (120 miles) away, but it was actually concealed behind the city, having already smashed the division of Re. The Hittites appeared just as Ramesses was setting up camp. Although

the Egyptians were greatly outnumbered, Ramesses led his troops courageously and held out until reinforcements arrived. The reconstruction below shows what the battle might have looked like.

Finally the Hittites and their allies were defeated, but the Egyptian army had suffered serious losses and had to return to Egypt in ruins. Nevertheless the account that Ramesses carved on the walls of many Egyptian temples describes an overwhelming victory, won single-handed.

Eventually fear of the Assyrians (see pages 74-75) brought the conflict to an end. In year 21, Ramesses signed a peace treaty with the Hittites.

The Battle of Kadesh

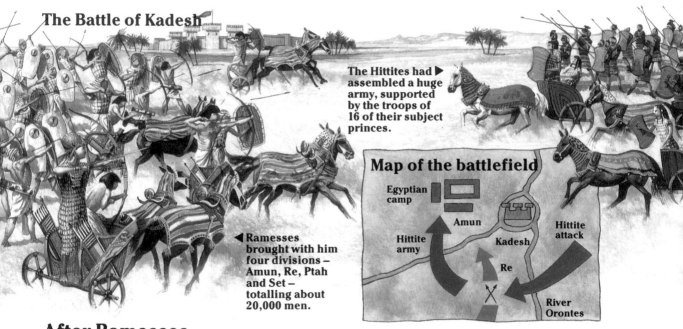

The Hittites had ▶ assembled a huge army, supported by the troops of 16 of their subject princes.

◀ Ramesses brought with him four divisions – Amun, Re, Ptah and Set – totalling about 20,000 men.

Map of the battlefield

Egyptian camp

Amun

Hittite army

Kadesh

Re

Hittite attack

River Orontes

After Ramesses

Ramesses reigned for so long that his 12 eldest sons died before him. He was succeeded by the 13th, Merenptah. Merenptah fought an invasion by Libyans and another by Sea Peoples (see opposite page). An inscription from his reign also mentions that the Egyptians had conquered the people of Israel. Merenptah maintained the spirit of his father's treaty with the Hittites, sending them grain during a severe famine. This is the first known record of international aid.

After Merenptah's death there was a period of confusion, as the descendants of Ramesses II competed with each other for the throne. Usurpers† seized power during the reign of Merenptah's son Seti II, who died without heirs. A Syrian may have taken control for a time, and for a brief period Tawosret†, sister-wife of Seti II, reigned alone as a 'king'. Dynasty XIX ended in turmoil.

Key dates: Dynasty XIX

1305-1186BC	Dynasty XIX
1305-1303BC	Reign of Ramesses I
1303-1289BC	Reign of Seti I
1289-1224BC	Reign of Ramesses II
1284BC	Battle of Kadesh
1270BC	Ramesses II makes a peace treaty with the Hittites. They agree to support each other in the event of attack by a third party.
1224-1204BC	Reign of Merenptah
1204-1200BC	Reign of Amenmesse
1200-1194BC	Reign of Seti II
1194-1188BC	Reign of Sitptah
1194-1186BC	Reign of Tawosret

These gold earrings were found in the tomb of the daughter of Seti II and Queen Tawosret.

*For a note about Egyptian dates, see page 65.
**For more about the organization of the Egyptian army, see pages 48-49.

Ramesses III and the Sea Peoples

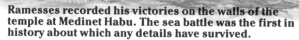

From the warring descendants of Dynasty XIX emerged Set-nakht, who became the founder of Dynasty XX. Although he may not have had the best claim to the throne, he was the strongest candidate. After a short reign, he was succeeded by his son Ramesses III. Ramesses was conscious of the weakness of his claim and attempted to

imitate the great Ramesses II, even naming his children after Ramesses' children.

The temple at Medinet Habu, built by Ramesses III

The Sea Peoples

In years 5 and 11*, poor harvests drove the Libyans to invade Egypt in search of new land. They were aided by people known as the Sea Peoples. This was the name the Egyptians gave to a loosely connected group of raiders and settlers from Greece, the Mediterranean islands and the west coast of Turkey. The Sea Peoples were first mentioned in texts in the reign of Amenhotep III. Driven by troubles in their homelands, they began by raiding around the Mediterranean. Later they brought their families with them and settled in areas that were already well-populated.

Sea Peoples travelling in carts

In year 8 a battle fleet of Sea Peoples cruised the eastern Mediterranean, capturing Cyprus and mainland coastal towns. Meanwhile an army was making its way south overland, accompanied by women and children riding in carts. After demolishing the Hittite empire, the Sea Peoples carried on towards Egypt, leaving a trail of ruined cities behind them.

As the army and fleet of Sea Peoples converged on Egypt, Ramesses gathered together all his resources to face the expected attack. Every man of military age was called up to fight; there were no reserves. Ramesses led his forces in two great battles, at sea and on land, and the Sea Peoples were finally defeated. This saved Egyptian civilization and changed the course of history in the Mediterranean (see pages 72-73).

Ramesses recorded his victories on the walls of the temple at Medinet Habu. The sea battle was the first in history about which any details have survived.

Problems at home

However, despite Ramesses' military successes, Egypt was in trouble. The eastern empire was now gone, and trade in the Mediterranean had been disrupted for years, depriving the country of much wealth. Prices rose rapidly, and signs of strain on the economy began to show. Several government officials were dismissed for dishonesty and incompetence. The wages of the royal tomb-builders were unpaid and the men went on the first recorded strike in history.

The harem conspiracy

Several of Ramesses' sons by his two chief queens died young, and there was a plot to kill him and put one of his sons by a minor wife on the throne. The conspirators, who included leading courtiers and soldiers, as well as members of the harem†, were caught and tried. The ring-leaders were condemned to death. Among the royal mummies of this period, archaeologists have found the body of a young man who had not been mummified. He had been bound, and put into his coffin alive. It is possible that this was the prince who had been involved in the plot.

Ramesses III was the last great warrior pharaoh. Eight more kings called Ramesses succeeded him, but their reigns were undistinguished and often short, and royal power declined (see page 73).

The royal tomb robberies

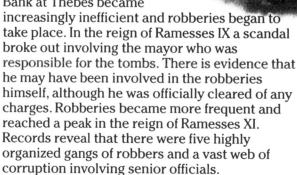

After Ramesses III's death, the guarding of the tombs on the West Bank at Thebes became increasingly inefficient and robberies began to take place. In the reign of Ramesses IX a scandal broke out involving the mayor who was responsible for the tombs. There is evidence that he may have been involved in the robberies himself, although he was officially cleared of any charges. Robberies became more frequent and reached a peak in the reign of Ramesses XI. Records reveal that there were five highly organized gangs of robbers and a vast web of corruption involving senior officials.

The world after the Sea Peoples

The attacks of the Sea Peoples (see page 71) brought about dramatic changes in the Mediterranean world. The destruction of the Hittites† left the way open for the rise of a new empire, that of the Assyrians (see pages 74-75), as well as a number of small independent states. Some Hittites headed south and formed new (Neo-Hittite) states, such as Carchemish, in the former southern provinces of the empire.

A group of nomads† called Aramaeans left the desert fringes and settled in fertile areas. They spread into Assyria and Babylonia and the area now called Syria, establishing independent cities such as Damascus. By 750BC Aramaic had become the language of international diplomacy.

In Greece, the civilization of Mycenae† soon collapsed and the Mycenaeans were replaced by the Phoenicians as the leading traders of the time.

What happened to the Sea Peoples?

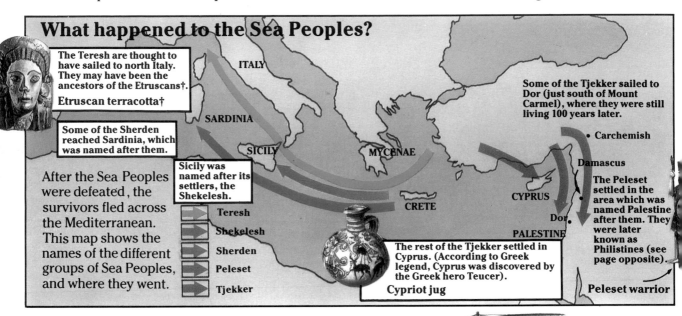

The Teresh are thought to have sailed to north Italy. They may have been the ancestors of the Etruscans†.

Etruscan terracotta†

Some of the Sherden reached Sardinia, which was named after them.

After the Sea Peoples were defeated, the survivors fled across the Mediterranean. This map shows the names of the different groups of Sea Peoples, and where they went.

Sicily was named after its settlers, the Shekelesh.

→ Teresh
→ Shekelesh
→ Sherden
→ Peleset
→ Tjekker

Some of the Tjekker sailed to Dor (just south of Mount Carmel), where they were still living 100 years later.

The Peleset settled in the area which was named Palestine after them. They were later known as Philistines (see page opposite).

The rest of the Tjekker settled in Cyprus. (According to Greek legend, Cyprus was discovered by the Greek hero Teucer).

Cypriot jug

Peleset warrior

The Phoenicians

The Sea Peoples destroyed some of the great cities of Canaan, like Ugarit (see page 25), but in coastal cities such as Byblos, Beirut, Sidon and Tyre, energetic merchants took over from the Mycenaeans as the leading traders of the Mediterranean. The inhabitants of these cities from about 1100BC are known as Phoenicians. The name is derived from *phoinix*, the Greek word for a purple dye, which was their most valuable export. The Phoenicians also exported cedarwood, glass and carved ivory, and carried cargo for other nations. They developed a simple alphabetic script which was later adapted by the Greeks and became the basis of our alphabet.

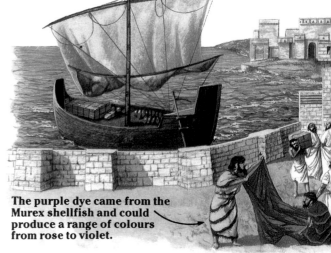

The purple dye came from the Murex shellfish and could produce a range of colours from rose to violet.

Map of Phoenician colonies

SPAIN
CORSICA
SARDINIA
Gades
Carthage
SICILY
NORTH AFRICA
Byblos
Beirut
Sidon
Tyre
■ Phoenician colonies

The Phoenicians were skilled sailors and explorers. They led an Egyptian expedition around Africa and set up trading colonies as far west as Gades (now Cadiz) in Spain, possibly as early as 1000BC. Their most famous colony was at Carthage in North Africa. The Carthaginians built a great harbour and fleet of ships. They later came into conflict with the Romans† over territorial rights in the Mediterranean.

The Philistines

The Philistines (formerly Peleset) were warriors and merchants who occupied the area known as Palestine. They dominated their neighbours, including the Israelites (see below), for nearly 200 years. The Philistines appear to have had some control over the local trade in iron, and some served as mercenaries in Egyptian frontier forts. They were led by the *Seren*, local princes who ruled from the five cities of Gaza, Ashkalon, Ashdad, Ekron and Gath.

Philistine decorated pottery was considered the finest in the region. Many of the designs reveal Mycenaean influence.

PALESTINE

Ekron
Ashdad
Ashkalon
Gath
Gaza

The tribes of Israel

The Israelites were a Semitic people who were divided into 12 tribes, led by men known as Judges. Experts believe that they were the first people to worship one God*. In about 1030BC, the Israelites went to Samuel, one of the Judges and the most important priest, asking him to appoint a king to lead them against the Philistines. Saul (c.1030-1010BC) was appointed king, and he was succeeded by David (c.1010BC-970BC).

David fought many wars, united his people, and turned Israel into a major power in the area. Jerusalem, which he captured in about 1005BC, became the capital city. Israelite power reached its height under Solomon (c.970-930BC). After his death, the kingdom split into two: Israel, with its capital at Shechem, and Judah, with its capital at Jerusalem.

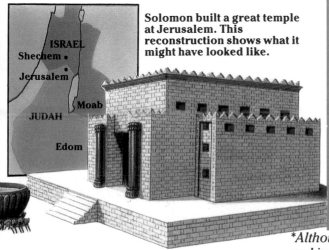

Solomon built a great temple at Jerusalem. This reconstruction shows what it might have looked like.

ISRAEL
Shechem
Jerusalem
Moab
JUDAH
Edom

The Third Intermediate Period

Royal power in Egypt declined after the reign of Ramesses III. High-ranking officials ruled the country and there was widespread corruption and incompetence. Libyans invaded and settled, Nubia broke away, and Egypt lost control of the eastern empire. By the end of the reign of Ramesses XI, real power rested with Heri-hor†, a general who became Vizier and High Priest of Amun. Heri-hor controlled Upper Egypt, and the Delta was governed by his son Smendes, who married Ramesses' daughter Princess Henttawy. Their descendants ruled from the Delta city of Tanis, as kings of Dynasty XXI, while the High Priests of Amun controlled Upper Egypt. The great days of the New Kingdom now gave way to the Third Intermediate Period (1069-664BC).

Coffin of Princess Maakare (c.1065-1045), daughter of a High Priest ▶ of Amun.

These gold vessels are from the ▲ royal burials of Dynasty XXI at Tanis.

Without an empire to control, the kings of Dynasty XXI concentrated on trade, but they were still capable of some military activity. To protect his trading interests, Pharaoh Si-Amun captured the Philistine city of Gaza and gave it as a dowry† to his daughter, who married King Solomon† of Israel.

Libyan influence increased. Shoshenq, a Libyan chief, married his son Osorkon to the Egyptian Princess Ma'at-ka-Re. In 945BC Shoshenq became king and founded Dynasty XXII. Family feuds led to civil wars and rival dynasties were set up. By 730BC there were five kings in Egypt.

In 728BC Egypt was conquered by a Nubian king called Piankhi† (or Piye), who united the country under Dynasty XXV. Having been ruled by Egypt for so long, the Nubians regarded themselves as the real heirs of Egyptian civilization and encouraged a revival of Egyptian culture. However, some Egyptian princes refused to accept them and supported an invasion by Assyrians.

This finally led to the Nubian retreat in 664BC. Prince Necho† of Sais, who was executed by the Nubians for his alliance with the Assyrians, was regarded by Egyptians as the first king of the next dynasty, Dynasty XXVI (see page 78), although he never ruled Egypt.

Piankhi's son, King Taharka (690-664BC)

Although Akhenaten† introduced the worship of one god in Egypt, this was abandoned after his reign.

73

The Assyrians

The original homeland of the Assyrians was a small area on the upper part of the River Tigris, around the cities of Ashur, Nineveh and Arbela. The area was culturally under the influence of its richer neighbours in Sumer and Akkad (see pages 6-8 and 24), and often under their political control as well.

However, some time before 2000BC, Assyria was invaded by large numbers of Semitic Amorites (see page 25), who established a line of kings. Under their leadership, the Assyrians built up a huge empire, which was at its greatest in the period known as the New Assyrian Empire (c.1000-612BC). They were an aggressive, militaristic people and made many enemies, among their neighbours as well as among their subjects. The empire was overthrown in 612BC by Medes and Babylonians (see pages 76-77).

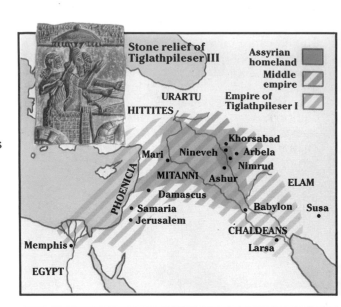

Stone relief of Tiglathpileser III

Assyrian homeland

Middle empire

Empire of Tiglathpileser I

URARTU
HITTITES
Khorsabad
Nineveh • Arbela
Mari • Nimrud
MITANNI Ashur
PHOENICIA ELAM
Damascus
Samaria • Babylon Susa
Jerusalem CHALDEANS
Memphis • Larsa
EGYPT

Assyrian cities

To reflect their power and success, the kings of the imperial age built themselves magnificent palaces and cities, such as Khorsabad and Nimrud. The walls of the palaces were decorated with painted stone reliefs†, which provide information about the lives of the Assyrians.

This is a reconstruction of the throneroom of Ashurnasirpal II at the palace at Nimrud.

Like the Sumerians, the Assyrians built ziggurats† for their gods.

Aqueducts† of mud-brick were built to provide a water supply for the palaces. The water was carried in a pipe with a waterproof lining of bitumen (tar) and stone. Arches carried the pipes across valleys.

Winged bulls with human heads feature in statues and reliefs found at Nimrud and Khorsabad.

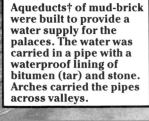

Hunting

Hunting appears to have been a great passion of the Assyrian kings. Lion hunts in particular seem to have had an almost religious significance.

Relief† showing a lion hunt

Ashur

Religion

The name Assyria comes from the chief god, Ashur, who gave his name to the main city. Many of the other important deities had Mesopotamian origins.

Warfare and empire-building

The Assyrians were tough warriors. From the earliest days they had to defend themselves against the Mesopotamians and hostile mountain tribes. From about 800BC, they introduced a series of military reforms and developed a formidable permanent army. Campaigns were now better organized and troops were well-equipped. Their weapons included bows, slings, swords, daggers, spears, battle axes and maces. Assyrian soldiers wore leather or chainmail armour and carried shields. Most soldiers fought on foot, but there were also chariot divisions.

The Assyrians were particularly good at besieging cities.

Scaling ladders were used for climbing walls.

For demolishing walls, they used cleverly shielded battering rams that protected the men operating them.

Camels

Some Assyrian reliefs show camels carrying goods or Arab† warriors into battle. Camels were probably first domesticated in about the 2nd millennium BC. They are better adapted than donkeys for desert journeys; they can carry twice as much, they do not need to feed and drink as frequently, and they can travel faster. This enabled people to cross long stretches of desert. This was especially useful for transporting goods from Arabia.

Stone relief showing camels

The Assyrians built good roads to ensure that the army could move quickly. The kings demanded annual tribute† from their subjects, and often collected it in person. If a city refused to pay, or if a conquered people rebelled, they were dealt with ruthlessly. The city and its surroundings were destroyed, and captives were tortured to death or made into slaves. Entire populations were sometimes deported to other parts of the empire. This deprived the rebels of resources and support, and was therefore an effective way of smashing their resistance. The Assyrians relied mainly on fear of punishment to keep the different provinces of their empire under control.

Key dates

c.2000-1450BC   The Old Assyrian Empire; during this period there is a very profitable trading relationship with Anatolia. This comes to an end with the expansion of the Hittites† in about 1500BC.

Assyrian merchants ▶ carried their goods on the backs of donkeys.

1813-1781BC   Reign of Shamshi-Adad, a great warrior who conquers an empire from Mari to Babylon. His son Ishme-Dagan is defeated by Rimsin of Larsa, and later becomes a vassal† of Hammurabi of Babylon (see page 25).

c.1450BC   Assyria passes under the control of the Mitannians (see page 44).

1363-1000BC   The Middle Assyrian Empire; Ashur-uballit I (1363-1328BC) restores Assyrian independence.

1273-1244BC   Reign of Shalmaneser I, who acquires the former eastern province of the Mitanni kingdom.

1114-1076BC   Reign of Tiglathpileser I, who makes great conquests. He marches west to the Mediterranean, campaigns against Aramaeans (see page 72) and Phrygians†, and encroaches on Babylonian territory.

c.1000-612BC The New Assyrian Empire; the greatest period of conquest and expansion.

Gold jewellery from Nimrud from the New Assyrian Empire

745-727BC   Reign of Tiglathpileser III, who conquers Damascus and Phoenicia.

726-722BC   Reign of Shalmaneser V, who conquers the kingdom of Israel (see page 73) and destroys the capital (which is now called Samaria). Many Israelites are deported to Mesopotamia and new people are brought in. They marry the few remaining Israelites, and their descendants are later known as Samaritans.

721-705BC   Reign of Sargon II†; he conquers the state of Urartu (between the Black and Caspian Seas) and builds a magnificent palace at Khorsabad.

704-681BC   Reign of Sennacherib†; he invades Egypt, but withdraws, and sacks Babylon in 689BC.

680-669BC   Reign of Esarhaddon†, who captures Memphis in Egypt.

668-627BC   Reign of Ashurbanipal II; he sacks Thebes (665BC), Babylon (648BC) and Susa (639BC).

614-612BC   Ashur and Nineveh fall to the Medes and Babylonians. By 608BC Assyria ceases to exist.

The Babylonians

The Kassite rulers of Babylon (see page 25) were thrown out in about 1158BC after a series of clashes with their neighbours, the Assyrians (see pages 74-75) and the Elamites†. After an unsettled period Babylonian rule was eventually restored and several short dynasties were established.

In the 7th century BC the Assyrians claimed control of Babylon and twice sacked the city for rebelling against their rule. In 627BC the Babylonians succeeded in overthrowing them,

with the help of the Medes (see opposite) and the Chaldeans, a group of Semitic† tribes who had settled on the coast of the Persian Gulf.

The New Babylonian (or Chaldean) Empire (626-539BC) was one of the greatest periods of Babylonian history. The Babylonians conquered a huge empire, which was at its height under Nebuchadnezzar II† (605-562BC). It was finally invaded by Persians in 539BC and absorbed into the Persian empire (see map opposite).

Babylon under Nebuchadnezzar II

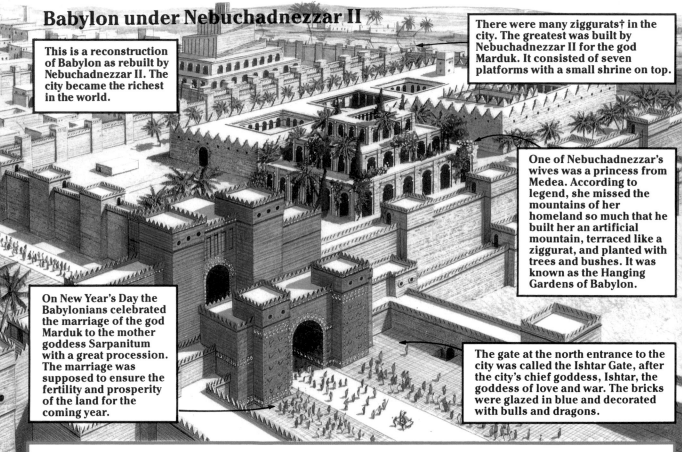

This is a reconstruction of Babylon as rebuilt by Nebuchadnezzar II. The city became the richest in the world.

There were many ziggurats† in the city. The greatest was built by Nebuchadnezzar II for the god Marduk. It consisted of seven platforms with a small shrine on top.

One of Nebuchadnezzar's wives was a princess from Medea. According to legend, she missed the mountains of her homeland so much that he built her an artificial mountain, terraced like a ziggurat, and planted with trees and bushes. It was known as the Hanging Gardens of Babylon.

On New Year's Day the Babylonians celebrated the marriage of the god Marduk to the mother goddess Sarpanitum with a great procession. The marriage was supposed to ensure the fertility and prosperity of the land for the coming year.

The gate at the north entrance to the city was called the Ishtar Gate, after the city's chief goddess, Ishtar, the goddess of love and war. The bricks were glazed in blue and decorated with bulls and dragons.

Key dates

1158-1027BC   Dynasty of Isin; the most notable king is Nebuchadnezzar I **(1126-1105BC)** who restores national pride after the sack of Babylon by the Kassites.

1026-1006   Dynasty of Sealand

1005-986BC   Dynasty of Bazi

985-980BC   Elamite Dynasty

979-732   Period known by historians as Dynasty "E"; the Babylonian Chronicles, a record of historical events and astronomical observations, is begun.

731-626BC   Ninth Dynasty; the Chaldeans and the Assyrians struggle for control of Babylon. The Chaldean leader Merodach-Baladin II† twice becomes king **(721-710BC and 703BC).** The Assyrians claim sovereignty and sack the city as a punishment for rebelling.

626-539BC   The Chaldean Dynasty or Neo (New) Babylonian Empire; Nabopolassar wins back Babylon, overthrows the Assyrians and takes over most of their land.

605-562BC   Reign of Nebuchadnezzar II

597BC   Nebuchadnezzar II occupies Jerusalem, capital of Judah (see page 73), and carries off many of its leading citizens to Babylon. After a revolt in **587-586BC** many Jews† are deported to Babylon and their descendants kept there until after the Persian conquest (see below). This is known as the Babylonian Captivity.

561-560BC   Reign of Evil-Merodach

559-556BC   Reign of Neriglissar

556-539BC   Reign of Nabonidus†

539BC   Babylon is taken over by the Persians (see opposite). They rule until **331BC,** followed by the Macedonians† **(330-307BC),** and the Seleucids† **(311-125BC).**

The Persians

In about 1500BC Aryan† tribes began settling in the area which is now named after them – Iran. Eventually one of these tribes, the Medes, emerged as the dominant group. By 670BC they had united under one kingdom, Medea, with a capital at Ecbatana. During the reign of Cyaxares, the Medes allied with the Babylonians (see opposite) and overthrew the Assyrian empire (see pages 74-75).

Another tribe, the Persians, established a rival kingdom under a ruling family called the Achaemenids in about 700BC. At first the Persians played a subordinate role to the Medes, but in 550BC Cyrus II† of Persia defeated his grandfather, King Astyages of Medea, and took over his lands. Cyrus went on to conquer the Kingdom of Lydia in 547-546BC and the Babylonian empire in 539BC. In 525BC Cyrus's son Cambyses II† conquered Egypt.

The Persian empire c.485BC

LYDIA
IONIA
MEDEA
• Ecbatana
ASSYRIA
• Susa
Babylon
PERSIA
EGYPT
• Persepolis
Gold armlet

Babylonian empire

Persian empire

Darius I

The empire reached its greatest extent under Darius I†. He was an able and successful ruler and established a fair and efficient code of laws. He divided the empire into provinces, known as 'satrapies', each run by a *satrap* (governor). A system of roads was built to link Persia to its far-flung provinces, and to enable soldiers and messengers to travel quickly and easily. Officials known as the 'King's Ears' went on regular tours of inspection, reporting directly back to the king. Subject peoples had to pay tribute† and to provide soldiers and ships for the army and navy.

Although the capital was at Susa, Darius I began building a huge palace complex at Persepolis.

Religion

The early Persians worshipped many deities. Their priests were famous for their skills as sorcerers; they were called *magi* (the origin of the word magic). One *magus* called Zarathustra (or Zoroaster) worshipped a single god, Ahura Mazda, who created all things. Evil was represented by the god's enemy, Angra Mainyu (or Ahriman).

The wars with Greece

Between 500BC and 494BC Greek colonists in Ionia (western Turkey) rebelled against their Persian rulers. They were helped by the city states of the Greek mainland. This provoked a series of wars between Greece and Persia which lasted from 490 to 449BC (see key dates below).

The Persian army had an elite regiment of 10,000 men known as the Immortals. Two of them are shown in this relief†.

The decline of the empire

From about 465BC the Persian empire was in decline. Its size made it difficult to govern and frequent revolts by subject peoples put a great strain on the government. Power struggles at court also undermined royal power. In Egypt there were a number of major revolts against the Persians, and the Egyptians eventually succeeded in winning independence from 404BC to 343BC.

The Persians were such unpopular rulers that in 336BC Alexander the Great† of Macedonia was able to lead his army into Egypt without resistance. By 330BC the whole of the Persian empire had come under his control.

Key dates

c.1500BC Aryan tribes begin settling in Persia.

c.700-600BC Kingdoms established in Medea and Persia.

550BC Cyrus II of Persia unites Persia and Medea under his rule. He conquers the empires of Lydia and Babylon.

525BC Cambyses II conquers Egypt.

522-485BC Reign of Darius I; the empire reaches its greatest extent.

500-494BC Greek colonists in Ionia rebel against Persia.

490BC Persians invade Greece and are defeated at the Battle of Marathon.

480-479BC Persians invade Greece; they win at Thermopylae and sack Athens, but are defeated at sea (Artemision, Salamis and Mykale), and on land (Plataea).

330BC Alexander the Great conquers the Persian empire.

The Late Period (Dynasties XXVI-XXX)

In 664BC, the Nubian kings (see page 73), were replaced by a native Egyptian dynasty (Dynasty XXVI). The new kings ruled from Sais and are sometimes called the Saite kings. The Assyrian invasions (see page 75) and discontent with Nubian rule had left Egypt poor, weak and divided, and it took the new pharaoh, Psamtek I, about nine years to assert his control over the whole land. He restored Egypt's independence from the Assyrians (who were still officially his overlords†), by stopping tribute† payments.

◀ **Psamtek I and the goddess Hathor**

Under the Saite kings, Egypt entered a new era of power, peace and prosperity, known as the Late Period. Industry and agriculture recovered and trade increased. In order to promote trade, foreigners were encouraged to settle in Egypt. Greek merchants set up colonies in Naucratis and Daphnae, and there was a flourishing Jewish colony in Elephantine. After the fall of Jerusalem in 587BC, many Jews† settled in the Delta.

Bronze men from the sea

Greek mercenaries† were hired by many Late Period kings. According to tradition, the goddess Wadjet promised the throne to Psamtek if he employed 'bronze men from the sea'. One day he saw some Greek soldiers who were shipwrecked off the Egyptian coast. Their bronze armour convinced him that these were the men described by the goddess. He employed them as mercenaries and went on to become king.

A Greek soldier

The God's Wife

During the Third Intermediate Period a princess was chosen to take the title 'God's Wife'. She never married, but instead devoted her life to the god Amun. The God's Wife was rich and powerful. She headed the priesthood of Amun and governed Upper Egypt on behalf of the king. Each God's Wife adopted a girl to succeed her, who was usually a daughter of the reigning king. At the start of Dynasty XXVI, the reigning God's Wife was a Nubian princess, Amenirdis II† (shown here).

Late Period art and culture

As the Egyptian economy improved, its art and culture rapidly recovered. In an attempt to regain their former greatness, the Egyptians tried to recreate the past. They studied old documents, repaired temples, revived ancient cults and copied the artistic styles of earlier periods.

During the Late Period wealthy people were buried in deep tomb-shafts in massive stone coffins called *sarcophagi*. The *sarcophagi* were decorated with pictures and texts, and usually had a portrait of the dead person on the lid. Inside the coffins archaeologists have sometimes found the mummy† covered with an elaborate beaded shroud†, like the one shown here.

Late Period mummy covering.

Meroë

Throughout this period Nubia was ruled by the descendants of the Nubian kings who had governed Egypt under Dynasty XXV. In the 6th century BC they abandoned their old capital, Napata, and moved south to Meroë. The Greeks called them *aithiops* (meaning 'dark-skinned'). This is the origin of the name Ethiopia, although modern Ethiopia lies south-east of Meroë. Meroitic culture was strongly influenced by Egypt, but it was also open to Greek and Indian influences. In the 3rd century BC the people of Meroë invented their own alphabetic script.

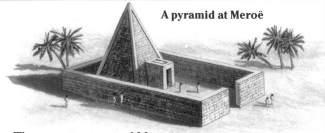

A pyramid at Meroë

The country around Meroë was greener, more fertile, and better irrigated than the Napata region. There were also large, valuable deposits of iron ore. The Meroitic people traded with Egypt, the Mediterranean, and with Arabia, East Africa and India, via the Red Sea.

Relations with Nubia

Although the Saite kings tried to maintain peace with Nubia, relations between the two countries were strained. The Egyptians resented their former conquerers, and cut out the names of the kings of Dynasty XXV from their monuments. After rumours of a Nubian attack, Psamtek II (595-589BC) invaded Nubia, marching as far south as Abu Simbel. Names carved on the walls by his Greek mercenaries can still be seen today.

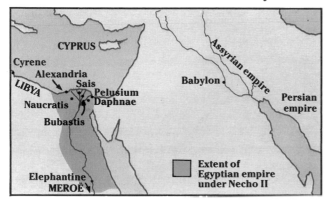

Extent of Egyptian empire under Necho II

Empire and exploration

There was a brief revival of Egypt's imperial role during the reign of Necho II (610-595BC). The Assyrian empire was under attack by Medes and Babylonians, and finally collapsed in 608BC. For a short period before the rise of Nebuchadnezzar II (see page 76), Necho was left in control of a large part of Egypt's former eastern empire.

Necho sent an expedition, led by Phoenician sailors, to explore the African coast. It became the first to sail around the entire continent of Africa.

Necho's expedition sailed down the Red Sea and round the Cape, returning to Egypt via the Straits of Gibraltar (then known as the Pillars of Herakles).

Bast

The popularity of the mother goddess Bast* (shown here) grew during the Late Period. The Greek historian Herodotus† described a festival at the goddess's city of Bubastis. He reported that people arrived by boat from all over Egypt and spent days and nights dancing, singing and feasting in her honour.

A revolt against the Greeks

Ordinary Egyptians resented the presence of large numbers of Greek merchants and soldiers in Egypt. This discontent erupted into a full-scale rebellion when King Apries thoughtlessly appeared in public in Greek armour, just after his army had been defeated by Greeks. Apries was deposed and executed, and the leader of the revolt, General Amasis, became king. However, although he reduced Greek trading privileges, he continued using Greek mercenaries and maintained friendly relations with Greece.

The Persian period

In 525BC, Amasis's son Psamtek III was defeated at the Battle of Pelusium by a new empire-builder, Cambyses† of Persia (see page 77). From 525BC to 404BC the Persians ruled Egypt as Dynasty XVII. They were unpopular rulers, and some showed no respect for Egyptian culture and religion. Rebellions broke out in the reign of Cambyses' grandson, Xerxes†. The Greeks (who were also enemies of the Persians) sent a fleet to help the rebels, and it took Xerxes six years to restore order.

In 404BC the Egyptians succeeded in gaining their independence under Dynasties XXVIII-XXX. The greatest kings of this period were Nectanebo I and Nectanebo II. They kept Egypt peaceful and prosperous and embarked on an ambitious building programme. In 343BC the country was reconquered by the Persians, who punished the Egyptians by plundering the land.

Alexander the Great

According to Egyptian legend, Alexander the Great (shown here) was the son of Nectanebo II, the last native Egyptian king. Nectanebo was said to have great magic powers, which he used one night to fly to Macedonia.

Between 334BC and 331BC the entire Persian empire was conquered by Alexander the Great†. He arrived in Egypt in 332BC, and was hailed as a liberator and accepted as pharaoh. He took care to respect Egyptian religion and culture and founded a new city, named Alexandria, on the Mediterranean coast. On his death in 323BC, his generals divided the empire between them. Egypt came under the control of General Ptolemy† who went on to found a new dynasty (see page 80).

For more about Bast and other Egyptian deities, see page 21.

The Ptolemies

At the death of Alexander the Great† in 323BC, Ptolemy† took over Egypt as *satrap* (governor). He ruled on behalf of Alexander's son, Alexander, and retarded brother, Philip Arrhideus. They were both murdered and in 305BC Ptolemy became pharaoh, founding a new dynasty. The Ptolemies became involved in struggles between Alexander's generals to divide up his empire, known as the Wars of the Diadochi (323-281BC). Later there were also quarrels with the Seleucids† over possession of Palestine, Phoenicia and southern Syria. Five bitter wars were fought (274-272BC, 260-253BC, 246-241BC, 221-217BC and 202-198BC) which ended with defeat for the Ptolemies.

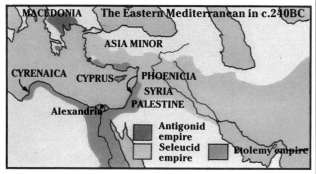

The Eastern Mediterranean in c.240BC

MACEDONIA
ASIA MINOR
CYRENAICA
CYPRUS
PHOENICIA
SYRIA
PALESTINE
Alexandria

Antigonid empire
Seleucid empire
Ptolemy empire

Alexandria

Alexandria, the new capital of Egypt founded by Alexander in 331BC, was designed like a Greek city, set out on a grid pattern. Alexander had intended it to be a great commercial and trading centre. Two magnificent harbours were built, which were capable of sheltering the largest ships of the day. Deep channels were dug linking the harbours to the River Nile.

The lighthouse on the island of Pharos was about 180m (70ft) tall. Its fire was reflected by mirrors and was visible 50km (30 miles) away.

A causeway 1.3km (almost a mile) long joined the lighthouse to the mainland.

Alexandria became a great centre of learning, and a number of important scientific inventions and discoveries were made there. The first two Ptolemies established the Museion (or Museum), a sort of research institute where some of the greatest scholars of the Greek world came to study. It contained a huge library, with about 500,000 papyrus scrolls. Ptolemy II commissioned a history of Egypt to be written, and the translations of Hebrew† scriptures into Greek.

Life under the Ptolemies

The economy flourished under the early Ptolemies. Large areas of marshland in the Fayum (see page 27) were drained and reclaimed for cultivation, trade was promoted and exports increased. However this new wealth only benefited the monarchs and their officials, who were mainly Greeks. In general, ordinary Egyptians were taxed heavily and exploited.

This relief† shows Ptolemy VII with two goddesses, Wadjet and Nekhbet.

The Ptolemies showed respect for Egyptian culture and religion. They built temples to the Egyptian gods, and had themselves shown on monuments in traditional Egyptian style. Greek gods soon became identified with Egyptian ones.

The decline of the dynasty

In the 2nd century BC, royal power began to decline. Feuds and murders became common within the royal family, and tensions between the Egyptians and the Greek immigrants erupted into violence. Upper Egypt broke away, and between 205BC and 185BC it was ruled by native pharaohs. During the reign of Ptolemy V, Macedonians and Seleucids invaded and almost succeeded in taking control. The period that followed was one of unrest, high inflation, heavy taxation and corrupt and inefficient government.

Cleopatra and the Romans

Despite the threat of the expanding Roman† empire, the Ptolemies did not give up hope of regaining the provinces they had lost to the Seleucids. Cleopatra VII† attempted to use her influence over the Roman dictator Julius Caesar†, who became her lover. After Caesar was murdered in 44BC, she married his friend Mark Antony†. In 31BC Antony and Cleopatra were defeated by Caesar's heir, Octavian, at the Battle of Actium. They committed suicide, and in 30BC Egypt became part of the Roman empire.

A Greek marble head of Cleopatra VII

Map of Ancient Egypt

• Çatal Hüyük

River Tigris

GREECE

ASIA MINOR

ANATOLIA

Hurran

TAURUS MOUNTAINS

Carchemish

MESOPOTAMIA

CRETE

CYPRUS

Ugarit

• Aleppo
Alalakh

SYRIA

• Qatna

Mari

River Euphrates

MEDITERRANEAN SEA

Byblos
Beiruit
Sidon
Tyre

• Damascus

• Hazor

Megiddo

River Jordan

Nile Delta

Ashdad
Ashkalon
Gaza

Ekron

Jerusalem

Alexandria   Sais   Buto
                        Tanis
Naucratis   Avaris   Pelusium
            Daphnae
        Bubastis
Gizah   Heliopolis
Sakkara   Memphis
It-towy
Meidum
THE FAYUM
Herakleopolis   Gerza

Gath

DEAD
SEA

LOWER EGYPT

SINAI

River Nile

EASTERN
DESERT

• Beni Hasan
• Tell el Amarna
(Akhetaten)

WESTERN DESERT

• Badari

Abydos   • Coptos
Thebes   Nagada
        Karnak

UPPER EGYPT

Hierakonpolis •

First Cataract   Aswan
Elephantine

RED SEA

Toshka
Abu Simbel
Buhen
Second Cataract

WAWAT

Semna

NUBIA

KUSH

Kerma   Third Cataract

Napata   Fourth Cataract

Egyptian empire at its
greatest extent during
the New Kingdom

Fifth Cataract

This map shows Ancient Egypt and the
surrounding area. Most of the the cities and
regions mentioned in the book can be found
here, if not elsewhere in the book. The shaded
area indicates the extent of the Egyptian empire at
its height during the New Kingdom.

Meroë

ETHIOPIAN
HIGHLANDS

81

The Egyptian kings

The list on these pages contains the names and approximate dates of most of the Egyptian kings up to the Roman conquest in 30BC. In some cases, particularly during the intermediate periods, several kings ruled simultaneously. Some kings are often known by the names the Greeks gave them. These are shown in brackets.

The Archaic Period (c.3100-2649BC)

DYNASTY I
Seven or eight kings starting with **Menes c.3100**

DYNASTY II
Eight or nine kings including **Hetepsekhemwy**, **Re'neb**, **Peribsen** and **Kha'sekhemui**

The Old Kingdom (c.2649-2150BC)

DYNASTY III

Sanakht	**c.2649-2630BC**
Zoser	**c.2630-2611BC**
Sekhemkhet	**c.2611-2603BC**
Kha'ba	**c.2603-2599BC**
Huni	**c.2599-2575BC**

DYNASTY IV

Sneferu	**c.2575-2551BC**
Khufu (Cheops)	**c.2551-2528BC**
Ra'djedef	**c.2528-2520BC**
Khafre (Khephren)	**c.2520-2494BC**
Menkaure (Mycerinus)	**c.2490-2472BC**
Shepseskaf	**c.2472-2467BC**

DYNASTY V

Userkaf	**c.2465-2323BC**
Sahure	**c.2458-2446BC**
Neferirkare	**c.2446-2426BC**
Shepseskare	**c.2426-2419BC**
Ra'neferef	**c.2419-2416BC**
Neuserre	**c.2416-2392BC**
Menkauhor	**c.2396-2388BC**
Djedkare	**c.2388-2356BC**
Unas	**c.2356-2323BC**

DYNASTY VI

Teti	**c.2323-2291BC**
Pepi I	**c.2289-2255BC**
Merenre	**c.2255-2246BC**
Pepi II	**c.2246-2152BC**
Nitocris**	**c.2152-2150BC**

First Intermediate Period (c.2150-2040BC)

DYNASTIES VII and VIII (c.2150-2134BC)
Many kings who reigned only for short periods

DYNASTIES IX and X (c.2134-2040BC)
The Herakleopolitan kings

The Middle Kingdom (c.2040-1640BC)

A line of kings reigned independently at Thebes, at the same time as the kings of Herakleopolis. This family later became Dynasty XI, ruling all Egypt under the Middle Kingdom.

DYNASTY XI

Mentuhotep II	**c.2040-2010BC**
Mentuhotep III	**c.2010-1998BC**
Mentuhotep IV	**c.1998-1991BC**

DYNASTY XII

Amenemhat I	**c.1991-1962BC**
Senusret I*	**c.1971-1926BC**
Amenemhat II*	**c.1929-1892BC**
Senusret II*	**c.1897-1878BC**
Senusret III*	**c.1878-1841BC**
Amenemhat III*	**c.1844-1797BC**
Amenemhat IV*	**c.1799-1787BC**
Sobek-neferu**	**c.1787-1783BC**

DYNASTY XIII (c.1783-1640BC)
About 70 kings most of whom had very short reigns

DYNASTY XIV
Princes from the Western Delta who broke away, ruling at the same time as Dynasty XIII

Second Intermediate Period (c.1640-1552BC)

DYNASTY XV
Hyksos kings including **Apophis (c.1585-1542BC)**

DYNASTY XVI
Minor Hyksos kings who ruled at the same time as Dynasty XV

DYNASTY XVII (c.1640-1552BC)
Fifteen Theban kings including **Tao I**, **Tao II** and **Kamose (c.1555-1552BC)**

The New Kingdom (1552-1069BC)

DYNASTY XVIII

Ahmose	**1552-1527BC**
Amenhotep I	**1527-1506BC**
Tuthmosis I	**1506-1494BC**
Tuthmosis II	**1494-1490BC**
Hatshepsut**	**1490-1468BC**
Tuthmosis III	**1490-1436BC**
Amenhotep II	**1438-1412BC**
Tuthmosis IV	**1412-1402BC**
Amenhotep III	**1402-1364BC**
Akhenaten (Amenhotep IV)	**1364-1347BC**
Smenkhare*	**1351-1348BC**
Tutankhamun	**1347-1337BC**
Ay	**1337-1333BC**
Horemheb	**1333-1305BC**

*These kings were crowned during the lifetime of the previous king.

**These are queens reigning as kings.

DYNASTY XIX

Ramesses I	1305-1303BC
Seti I	1303-1289BC
Ramesses II	1289-1224BC
Merenptah	1224-1204BC
Amenmesse	1204-1200BC
Seti II	1200-1194BC
Siptah	1194-1188BC
Tawosret**	1194-1186BC

DYNASTY XX

Set-nakht	1186-1184BC
Ramesses III	1184-1153BC
Ramesses IV	1153-1146BC
Ramesses V	1146-1142BC
Ramesses VI	1142-1135BC
Ramesses VII	1135-1129BC
Ramesses VIII	1129-1127BC
Ramesses IX	1127-1109BC
Ramesses X	1109-1099BC
Ramesses XI	1099-1069BC

Third Intermediate Period (1069-664BC)

DYNASTY XXI

Smendes I	1069-1043BC
Amenemnisu	1043-1039BC
Psusennes I	1039-991BC
Amenemope	993-984BC
Osochor	984-978BC
Si-Amun	978-959BC
Psusennes II	959-945BC

DYNASTY XXII

Shoshenq I	945-924BC
Osorkon I	924-889BC
Shoshenq II	c.890BC
Takeloth I	889-874BC
Osorkon II	874-850BC
Takeloth II	850-825BC
Shoshenq III	825-773BC
Pimay	773-767BC
Shoshenq V	767-730BC
Osorkon IV	730-715BC

DYNASTY XXIII
A separate line of kings ruling at the same time as the later kings of Dynasty XXII

DYNASTY XXIV
Ruling at the same time as Dynasties XXII and XXIII

Tefnakhte I	727-720BC
Bakenranef	720-715BC

DYNASTY XXV
The Nubian kings

Piankhi	728-716BC
Shabako	716-702BC
Shebitku	702-690BC
Taharka	690-664BC
Tanut-Amun	664-663BC

The Late Period (664-332BC)

DYNASTY XXVI
The Saite kings

Psamtek I	664-610BC
Necho II	610-595BC
Psamtek II	595-589BC
Apries	589-570BC
Amasis	570-526BC
Psamtek III	526-525BC

DYNASTY XXVII (525-404BC)
The Persian kings including
Cambyses (525-521BC), **Darius I (521-485BC)**
and **Xerxes (485-464BC)**.

DYNASTY XXVIII

Amyrtaeus	404-c.399BC

DYNASTY XXIX

Nepherites I	c.399-393BC
Achoris	c.393-380BC
Psammuthis	c.380-379BC
Nepherites II	c.379

DYNASTY XXX

Nectanebo I	c.379-361BC
Tachos	c.361-359BC
Nectanebo II	c.359-342BC

DYNASTY XXXI (341-323BC)
The second period of Persian kings

The Macedonian kings (332-305BC)

Alexander the Great	332-323BC
Philip Arrhidaeus	323-316BC
Alexander IV	316-305BC

The Ptolemies (305-30BC)

Ptolemy I	305-284BC
Ptolemy II	284-246BC
Ptolemy III	246-221BC
Ptolemy IV	221-205BC
Ptolemy V	205-180BC
Ptolemy VI	160-164BC and 163-145BC
Ptolemy VII	145BC
Ptolemy VIII	170-163BC and 145-116BC
Queen Cleopatra III and Ptolemy IX	116-107BC
Queen Cleopatra III and Ptolemy X	107-88BC
Ptolemy IX	88-81BC
Queen Cleopatra Berenice	81-80BC
Ptolemy XI	80BC
Ptolemy XII	80-58BC
Queen Berenice IV	58-55BC
Ptolemy XII	55-51BC
Queen Cleopatra VII	51-30BC

with Ptolemy XIII (51-47BC), with Ptolemy XIV (47-44BC)
and with Ptolemy XV (44-30BC)

83

Who was who in Egypt and the Middle East

Below is a list of important people from Egypt, Mesopotamia and other early civilizations in the Middle East. If a person's name appears in bold in the text of an entry, that person also has his or her own entry in this list. Dates of reigns, where known, are shown in brackets.

Ahhotep I. Queen of Egypt (Dynasty XVII). Daughter of Tao I and **Teti-sheri**, and sister-wife of **Tao II**. She acted as regent† during the reign of her son **Ahmose**.

Ahmes Nefertari. Queen of Egypt (Dynasty XVIII). Daughter of **Tao II** and **Ahhotep I**, and sister-wife of **Ahmose**. She held the offices of God's Wife† and of Second Prophet of Amun in the temple at Karnak and acted as regent† for her fourth son, Amenhotep I. Together they founded the community of royal tomb-builders, who eventually settled in the village at Deir el Medinah (see page 66).

Ahmose (1552-1527BC). King of Egypt. The first king of Dynasty XVIII and the New Kingdom. Son of **Tao II** and **Ahhotep I**, he came to the throne while still a child, with his mother as regent†. Ahmose continued the war begun by his father and brother and succeeded in liberating Egypt from the Hyksos†. After suppressing rebellions at home, he began the reconquest of Nubia.

Ahmose of El Kab (Dynasty XVII/XVIII). Egyptian soldier in the army of King **Ahmose**. He fought on campaigns to drive the Hyksos† from Egypt and won the 'Gold of Valour', the highest award for bravery. The biography on the walls of his tomb is an important source of information about the wars against the Hyksos.

Akhenaten/Amenhotep IV (1364-1347BC). King of Egypt (Dynasty XVIII). One of the most controversial figures in ancient history. He abandoned the traditional Egyptian deities and introduced the worship of one god, the disc of the sun, known as the Aten. He changed his name to Akhenaten and built a new capital, Akhetaten. After his death all these changes were reversed and the capital was abandoned. Akhenaten's monuments were destroyed and he himself was branded as a heretic†.

Alexander the Great (356-323BC). King of Macedonia, military leader and empire-builder. After taking control of Greece, he marched into Asia Minor and conquered the entire Persian empire (including Egypt). He founded many new cities, the most famous of which was the port of Alexandria in Egypt, which became the new capital. Alexander married a Persian princess called Roxane and died in Babylon at the age of 32. His heirs were eventually murdered and the empire was divided up between his generals, one of whom, **Ptolemy**, became King of Egypt and founded the Ptolemaic Dynasty.

Amenemhat I (c.1991-1962BC). First king of Dynasty XI. In order to secure the succession, he had his son Senusret I crowned in his own lifetime. Amenemhat was eventually murdered, but Senusret remained in control.

Amenhotep IV, see **Akhenaten**.

Amenhotep, son of Hapu (Reign of Amenhotep III). Egyptian royal scribe. He held some of the highest offices in the land and statues of him were erected in the temples of Amun and Mut at Karnak. He was worshipped as a god in the Late Period in Thebes.

Amenirdis II. Nubian princess and God's Wife. Daughter of King **Taharka** (Dynasty XXV). She was obliged to adopt as her heir **Nitocris**, the daughter of Psamtek I, the first king of Dynasty XXVI.

Ankhesenamun. Queen of Egypt (Dynasty XVIII). Sister-wife of **Tutankhamun**. After his death she was married to Ay, an elderly courtier who became king.

Antony, Mark (82-30BC). Roman soldier and politician. Lover of **Cleopatra VII**, he ruled Egypt with her after the death of **Caesar**. After a quarrel with Caesar's heir Octavian, war broke out; Antony and Cleopatra were defeated at the Battle of Actium and committed suicide.

Apophis. One of the greatest of the Hyksos† kings of Egypt (Dynasty XVI). During his reign war broke out with **Tao II**, the King of Thebes. This led to the expulsion of the Hyksos and the start of the New Kingdom.

Bay. An adventurer of Syrian origin who became influential in Egypt at the end of Dynasty XIX. He tried to sieze the throne after the death of Queen **Tawosret**.

Bint-Anath. Queen of Egypt (Dynasty XIX). Daughter and wife of **Ramesses II**. She has a tomb in the Valley of the Queens on the West Bank at Thebes.

Caesar, Julius (c.100-44BC). Roman politician, writer and general who was made dictator for life. He intervened in a quarrel between his lover **Cleopatra VII** and her brother and secured the Egyptian throne for her. He was murdered on 15 March 44BC.

Cambyses (530-522BC). King of Persia. Son of Cyrus II. He conquered Egypt in 525BC. He appears to have been a cruel man, and the Greek historian **Herodotus** claimed that he was mad. According to one story, he broke into the tomb of a pharaoh and burned the corpse. He is said to have offended the Egyptians by desecrating temples and wounding the Apis bull†. Cambyses died on his return to Persia in 522BC, and was succeeded by his cousin **Darius**.

Cleopatra VII (51-30BC). Queen of Egypt (Ptolemaic Period). Sister-wife of both Ptolemy XIII and Ptolemy XIV and lover of the Roman dictator **Julius Caesar**. She later married his friend **Mark Antony**. Antony and Cleopatra were defeated at the Battle of Actium (31BC) by Caesar's heir Octavian. In 30BC Cleopatra committed suicide and Egypt was absorbed into the Roman empire.

Cyrus II (559-529BC). King of Persia and founder of the Achaemenid Dynasty. In 550BC Cyrus defeated his grandfather Astyages of Medea and united the two kingdoms under his rule. He defeated King Croesus of Lydia in 547-546BC and annexed his empire, and in 539BC he conquered the Babylonian empire.

Darius the Great (522–485BC). King of Persia. Under him the Persian empire reached its greatest extent. An able and successful ruler, he established a fair and efficient code of laws and divided the empire into provinces, each run by a *satrap* (or governor).

Elissa or **Dido**. Queen of Carthage. Princess of the Phoenician city of Tyre, and niece of Queen Jezebel, wife of King Ahab of the Israelites†. She fled with her brother to north Africa and built the city of Carthage. According to Roman tradition, the Greek hero Aeneas landed there after the destruction of Troy. Dido fell in love with him and committed suicide when he left.

Esarhaddon (680–667BC). King of Assyria. He gained the support of the Babylonians by rebuilding the city of Babylon, which had been destroyed by his father **Sennacherib**. However elsewhere he faced great problems. The empire was huge and the cruelty of the Assyrians made them unpopular with their subjects. In 671BC Esarhaddon invaded the Nile Delta and Assyrian governors were installed in Egypt.

Hammurabi (c.1792–1750BC). King of Babylon. He extended the frontiers of the kingdom and built up an empire which included all of Sumer and Akkad. A gifted administrator, he was concerned with law and order and established a unified system of laws and penalties.

Hatshepsut (1490–1468BC). Queen of Egypt (Dynasty XVIII). Daughter of Tuthmosis I and Queen Ahmose and sister-wife of Tuthmosis II. Although appointed regent† for his son **Tuthmosis III**, she took power and reigned as "king" for over 20 years. Evidence of her reign is scarce, as Tuthmosis destroyed her official inscriptions.

Hekanakhte. Egyptian priest (Dynasty XI). Letters and documents found in his tomb provide important information on the running of a large household and estate, as well as an insight into tensions and intrigues in a wealthy family.

Heri-hor. Egyptian soldier (Dynasty XX). A member of a family of officials which became influential as the power of the pharaohs declined. During the reign of Ramesses XI, Heri-hor took control of Upper Egypt. Lower Egypt was governed by his son Smendes, who married a daughter of Ramesses XI. When Ramesses died, Smendes became the first king of Dynasty XXI.

Herodotus (c.460–420BC). Greek historian, often called "the Father of History". He wrote a history of the Greeks which centred around the Persian Wars. He was one of the first writers to compare historical facts and to see them as a sequence of linked events.

Hetepheres I. Queen of Egypt (Dynasty III). Daughter of Huni, sister-wife of **Sneferu** and mother of **Khufu**. Shortly after her burial, the tomb was robbed and her body destroyed. Khufu had the remains of her burial moved to Gizah, where it was discovered this century. Although the wooden furniture had crumbled, archaeologists were able to reconstruct it from the surviving gold foil that covered it.

Hiram. King of the Phoenician city of Tyre. Contemporary with King David and King Solomon of the Israelites†. He supplied cedar and fir trees for Solomon's temple at Jerusalem and sent craftsmen to work in bronze.

Horemheb. King of Egypt (Dynasty XVIII). General and regent† during the reign of **Tutankhamun**. He appears to have had no claim to the throne except as husband of Ay's daughter **Mutnodjmet**.

Imhotep. Egyptian official (Dynasty III). Architect of the first pyramid, the step pyramid of King **Zoser** at Sakkara. He was also a doctor and a high priest and may have been involved in introducing the calendar. Later generations worshipped him as a god, and the Greeks identified him with their god of medicine, Asclepius.

Kamose (c.1555–1550). King of Egypt (Dynasty XVII: the Theban kings). Son of **Tao II** and **Ahhotep I**. He fought with the Hyksos† and extended his frontier as far as north the Fayum. He died in battle and was succeeded by his brother **Ahmose**.

Khufu or **Cheops** (c.2551–2528BC). King of Egypt (Dynasty IV). Son of **Sneferu** and **Hetepheres I**. His pyramid, the Great Pyramid at Gizah, is the largest ever built and was the oldest of the seven wonders of the ancient world. The diorite quarries at Toshka in Nubia were first mined during his reign and a fortified town was built as a trade centre at Buhen.

Meket-re. High-ranking Egyptian official in the reign of Mentuhotep III. His tomb on the West Bank at Thebes contained a magnificent set of tomb models, including models of his villa with its garden and pool, kitchens, workshops, cattle, granaries and boats.

Menes (c.3100BC). King of Upper Egypt. He conquered Lower Egypt and united the two kingdoms, so becoming the first king of Dynasty I. He may have married a princess from Lower Egypt, giving their son Hor-aha a hereditary claim to the whole of Egypt.

Mentuhotep II (c.2061–2010BC). King of Thebes in Upper Egypt (Dynasty XI). In about 2040BC he defeated the King of Lower Egypt (Dynasty X) and reunited the country. This began the Middle Kingdom.

Merodach-Baladin (or **Marduk-apal-iddina**). Chaldean prince from Sumer and champion of Babylonian independence, he challenged the powerful **Sargon II** of Assyria. He became King of Babylon between 721BC and 711BC, but was driven out by Sargon and forced to flee to Elam. After Sargon's death in 705BC, he returned to Babylon, but was expelled the following year. He fled to the marshes and waged guerilla war on the Assyrians. He died in exile in Elam.

Montu-em-het. An Egyptian official from an influential Theban family (Dynasty XXV). He married the granddaughter of one of the Nubian kings and became the most important official in Thebes. When the Assyrians invaded Egypt in 665BC, he fled to Nubia with King Tanut-Amun. He returned to Egypt when a new Egyptian dynasty (Dynasty XXVI) was established.

85

Mutnodjmet. Queen of Egypt (Dynasty XVIII). Daughter of Ay, a courtier who became pharaoh. She married a general called **Horemheb**, who became the next king.

Nabonidus (556-539BC). King of Babylon. An official of royal descent, he came to the throne during a period of turmoil after the death of **Nebuchadnezzar II**. He commissioned a lot of rebuilding in Sumer and studied in archives to discover how earlier buildings had been constructed. After leaving his son Belshazzar in control in Babylon, he withdrew to Arabia for several years, possibly in an attempt to secure control of the lucrative trading route from southern Arabia. When the Persians attacked Babylon he returned home, but he and his son were killed and the Babylonian empire came to an end.

Naram-Sin (c.2291-2255BC). King of Akkad. Grandson of **Sargon**. He attempted to rebuild Sargon's empire and succeeded in extending the frontiers west as far as Lebanon. The empire disintegrated after his death.

Nebuchadnezzar II (605-562BC). King of Babylon. Under him Babylon was rebuilt and the New Babylonian Empire reached its height. He captured the provinces of Syria and Palestine and dealt severely with his new vassals† when they failed to pay tribute†. In 597BC he conquered Jerusalem and carried off 3000 of its leading inhabitants. The King of Judah revolted in 587BC. After an 18 month siege the walls and temple of Jerusalem were destroyed and the people carried off to Babylon.

Necho I (672-664BC). Prince of Sais (Lower Egypt). Necho's family had never accepted the Nubian kings of Dynasty XXV. When the Assyrians invaded Egypt in 664BC Necho sided with them. He was appointed governor by the Assyrians, but was captured and executed by the Nubians. His son Psamtek escaped and returned to restore Egypt's independence as the founder of Dynasty XXVI. However the Egyptians regarded Necho as the first king of their new dynasty and for this reason he is known as Necho I.

Nefertari. Chief queen of **Ramesses II** (Dynasty XIX). One of the temples at Abu Simbel was built for her, as well as a tomb in the Valley of the Queens.

Nefertiti. Queen of Egypt (Dynasty XVIII). Wife of **Akhenaten** and mother of **Ankhesenamun**.

Nitocris (or **Net-ikerty**). God's Wife†. Daughter of Psamtek I, first king of Dynasty XXVI. She helped reconcile Upper Egypt to the new dynasty.

Nitocris. Queen of Egypt (Dynasty VI). Daughter of **Pepi II**. The direct male line appears to have died out soon after her father's death and Nitocris ruled on her own for about two years (c.2152-2150BC).

Pepi II (c.2246-2252BC). King of Egypt (Dynasty VI). He reigned for 94 years; the longest recorded reign in history. After his death disputes broke out over the succession. Egypt collapsed into civil conflict and confusion and the Old Kingdom came to an end.

Piankhi (747-716BC). King of Nubia and Egypt. He saw himself as the guardian of Egyptian culture and religion during a period of decadence and political division in Egypt. He conquered Egypt in 728BC, and became the first king of Dynasty XXV. He died in Nubia and is buried under a pyramid at el Kurru.

Ptolemy I (305-284BC). King of Egypt. A general in the army of **Alexander the Great**, he was appointed governor of Egypt after Alexander's death, ruling on behalf of Alexander's son and retarded brother. When they were both murdered Ptolemy became king and founder of the Ptolemaic dynasty.

Ramesses II (1289-1224BC). King of Egypt (Dynasty XIX). One of the best known kings in Egyptian history. Ramesses built a large number of fortresses, temples and monuments, including two temples cut into the rock face at Abu Simbel. During the early part of his reign he was engaged in a struggle with the Hittites. Eventually fear of the Assyrians brought an end to the conflict and peace was made between the two sides.

Ramose. Vizier of Upper Egypt during the reigns of **Amenhotep III** and **Akhenaten**. A member of the successful family of **Amenhotep, son of Hapu**.

Rekhmire. Vizier of Upper Egypt (reign of **Tuthmosis III**). His tomb at Thebes contains valuable scenes of daily life, as well as a text which describes the instructions given by the king to the Vizier on his appointment to office.

Sargon of Akkad (c.2371-2316BC). A gifted soldier and administrator, he united Akkad and Sumer under his rule and built up the first great empire in Mesopotamia. The empire fell apart after his death, but was reconquered by his grandson **Naram-Sin**.

Sargon II (721-705BC). King of Assyria. A brilliant and ruthless soldier, he conquered the state of Urartu and built a magnificent palace at Khorsabad.

Sennacherib (704-681BC). King of Assyria. The favourite son of **Sargon II**. During his reign there were constant revolts in Babylon, led by **Merodach-Baladin**. These ended when the Assyrians sacked Babylon in 689BC. The kings of Sidon, Ashkalon, Judah and Ekron also rebelled, encouraged by the King of Egypt. After defeating the rebels, Sennacherib invaded Egypt, but the Egyptians were saved by the sudden withdrawal of the Assyrian army after an outbreak of plague. Sennacherib was murdered by one of his sons who crushed him with a statue of a god.

Senusret III (c.1878-1841BC). King of Egypt (Dynasty XII). He led several campaigns against the Kushites who were threatening the frontiers of Egypt's Nubian province (established at the Second Cataract†). He also began a massive rebuilding programme to strengthen the fortresses there, and dug a channel through the rocks of the First Cataract, so that ships could sail directly upstream. Senusret claimed to have established his frontier further south than any previous king had done.

Sheba, Queen of. Sheba, or Saba, was a rich, fertile land on the south coast of Arabia. The Shebans were situated on a good trading route from Africa and the East and traded agricultural produce and incense. According to the Bible, the Queen of Sheba travelled north to visit **Solomon**, King of the Israelites†. According to Ethiopian tradition, she had a son by him, from whom the Ethiopian royal family are descended. Muslim sources give her name as Bilqis.

Shuppiluliuma (c.1380-1340BC). King of the Hittites. The greatest king of the Hittite New Kingdom; a wily and able ruler and diplomat and a successful soldier. Under him the Hittite empire reached its greatest extent. In about 1370BC he conquered the Mitannian empire and then encouraged discontented Egyptian vassals† to rebel. When **Tutankhamun** died, his young widow **Ankhesenamun** wrote to him, offering to marry one of his sons and make him King of Egypt. Shuppiluliuma eventually sent one of his sons to Egypt, but the plot was discovered and the Hittite prince was murdered. To avenge his son, he attacked the northern provinces of the Egyptian empire in Syria.

Sinuhe. Egyptian army officer (Dynasty XII). On a campaign against the Libyans, he heard that King **Amenemhat I** had been murdered, and that there was a plot to deprive his son Senusret of the throne. For some unknown reason, Sinuhe fled in panic to Syria, where he stayed for many years. After numerous adventures he returned home. His story is inscribed on the walls of his tomb and was copied and turned into a book.

Sneferu (c.2575-2551BC). King of Egypt (Dynasty III). Son of Huni and a secondary wife, he became king after the premature death of the heir. In order to strengthen his claim, he married his half-sister, **Hetepheres I**. Sneferu appears to have been tough, efficient and ruthless. He sent an expedition to Nubia and many Nubians were killed and others taken prisoner. Sneferu built himself two pyramids – the 'Bent' Pyramid and the Northern Pyramid (the first to be designed and completed as a straight-sided pyramid).

Sobek-neferu (c.1787-1783BC). Queen of Egypt (Dynasty XII). With the death of her brother Amenemhat IV the direct male line of Dynasty XII died out and she ruled alone for four years.

Solomon (c.970-930BC). King of the Israelites†. Son of David. He built a great temple at the capital, Jerusalem, and Israelite power reached its height. After Solomon's death the kingdom split into two: Israel and Judah.

Taharka (690-664BC). King of Egypt (Dynasty XXV: the Nubian kings). Son of **Piankhi**. The Assyrians attacked Egypt three times during Taharka's reign. The second invasion reached Memphis, but he escaped to Nubia and later returned. In the third invasion the Assyrians were supported by Egyptian princes such as **Necho of Sais**. Taharka again fled to Nubia, and a new native Egyptian dynasty was established.

Tao II. King of Thebes (Dynasty XVII). Son of Tao I and **Teti-sheri**. During his reign the Thebans began plotting to drive out the Hyksos† who were ruling Egypt from Avaris as Dynasty XV. War broke out between them and Tao succeeded in pushing his frontier north to Assiut.

Tawosret (c.1194-1186BC). Queen of Egypt (Dynasty XIX). Daughter of Merenptah and sister-wife of Seti II. After Merenptah's death, Amenmesse (a member of the royal family) seized the throne briefly before Seti took control. When Seti died Amenmesse's son Siptah was made ruler. Tawosret married him and when he died she reigned as a "king" until her death three years later.

Teti-sheri. Queen of Thebes (Dynasty XVII). Wife of Tao I. She appears to have been a woman of great influence who may have encouraged the men of her family into rebellion against the Hyksos†. The Hyksos were finally driven out by her grandson **Ahmose**, and he provided her with estates recaptured from them, a burial at Thebes and a monument at Abydos.

Tia. Egyptian princess (Dynasty XIX). Eldest daughter of Seti I and sister of **Ramesses II**. She married a high-ranking official and is buried with him at Sakkara. The marriage probably took place before her grandfather, Ramesses I, founded Dynasty XIX. Otherwise she would probably have married her brother Ramesses II.

Tiy. Queen of Egypt (Dynasty XVIII). Daughter of two influential courtiers called Tuyu and Yuya. Wife of Amenhotep III (who may also have been her cousin) and mother of **Akhenaten**.

Tutankhamun (1347-1337BC). King of Egypt (Dynasty XVIII). Son of **Akhenaten**. He came to the throne aged only about nine and married his half-sister **Ankhesenamun**. A general called **Horemheb** and a courtier called Ay became regents†. Although Tutankhamun died young, he is famous because of the treasures found in the 1920s in his tomb in the Valley of the Kings. Many of the tombs of the Dynasty XVIII kings had been repeatedly robbed over the centuries, but Tutankhamun's tomb had escaped attention.

Tuthmosis III (1490-1436BC). King of Egypt (Dynasty XVIII). Son of Tuthmosis II and nephew of **Hatshepsut**, who was regent† and kept him from power for the first twenty years of his reign. Tuthmosis was probably the greatest of the warrior pharaohs of the New Kingdom. He enlarged the Egyptian empire to its widest limits.

Xerxes (485-465BC). King of Persia. Son of **Darius**. He put down a revolt in Egypt and spent much of his reign fighting the Greeks. He invaded Greece in 480BC, won a battle at Thermopylae and sacked Athens. His forces were later defeated at Salamis and Plataea.

Zoser (c.2630-2611BC). King of Egypt (Dynasty III). The first pyramid, the step pyramid at Sakkara, was designed as a tomb for him by his architect **Imhotep**.

Glossary

Many foreign or unfamiliar words in this book are listed and explained in the glossary below. The names of peoples are also included. Other words related to the term appear in bold within the text of the entry. When a word in the text of an entry is followed by a dagger, that word has its own entry in this list. When the sign follows a name, see the 'Who's who' that begins on page 84.

Alabaster. A translucent, white stone veined rather like marble. It was used for decorative features, such as floors in temples, and for items such as vases and lamps in wealthy Egyptian households.

Amulet. A small figure of a god or goddess or a sacred object. Amulets were worn as charms for luck and protection by the living and the dead. Examples include the *ankh*†, the *djed*-pillar†, and the scarab beetle.

Ankh. An Egyptian amulet†; the symbol of life.

Aryan. A term used to refer to the language or people of the Iranian and Indian branches of the Indo-European† group.

Aqueduct. A man-made channel for tranporting water.

Arab. A member of a group of Semitic† people living in Arabia and neighbouring territory.

Bedouin. Nomads† inhabiting the deserts of North Africa and Arabia.

Caravan. A group of people, usually merchants, travelling together for safety across a desert.

Caste system. A hereditary system of rigidly defined social classes in India. Now a social system, but originally based on professions.

Cataract. A place where large rocks block the path of the River Nile. Cataracts often formed important boundaries in ancient times.

Concubine. A term applied in a historical context to a woman who lived with a man without being married. In Egypt it was an officially recognized relationship and a concubine had special rights.

City state. A self-governing city with its surrounding territory, forming the basis for an independent state.

Cult. The worship of a particular god or goddess, or the practice of a particular system of religious rites. Most Egyptian gods and goddesses had a home town where their main temple, known as a **cult temple**, was situated. The temple was the home of the **cult statue**, which was thought to be the means by which the deity could communicate with the outside world.

Djed-pillar. An Egyptian amulet† representing stability and continuity of power.

Dowry. Money or property brought by a woman to her husband at the time of marriage.

Dynasty. A succession of hereditary rulers. Dynasties are often referred to by a family name. Egyptian dynasties are numbered I to XXXI.

Elamites. A people from Elam, a land east of the River Tigris. The Elamites destroyed the Sumerian city of Ur in about 2000BC. Elam itself was absorbed into the empire of Sargon† of Akkad.

Faience. A type of glazed earthenware, made by heating powdered quartz.

First Cataract. See **Cataract**.

Fourth Cataract. See **Cataract**.

God's Wife. Head of the priestesses at the temple of Amun at Karnak. By the Third Intermediate Period this was a very powerful position held by a princess.

Harem. The name given to the part of an Oriental (usually Muslim) house reserved strictly for women (wives and concubines†). It is used to describe the part of an Egyptian palace where the royal women lived.

Hebrew. An ancient Semitic† language and people. The people are also known as Israelites† and Jews†.

Heretic. A person who maintains a set of beliefs contrary to and condemned by the established religion. The beliefs held by a heretic are described as **heretical** and the person is said to be guilty of **heresy**.

Hieroglyphics. The Egyptian system of writing in which pictures or signs are used to represent objects, ideas or sounds. The pictures themselves are known as **hieroglyphs**.

Hittites. An Indo-European† people from Anatolia, who built up a great empire in Asia Minor and northern Syria in the second millenium BC.

Hyksos. A group of Semitic† peoples, probably mostly nomads†, who invaded and conquered Egypt during the Second Intermediate Period.

Indo-European. A group of languages which includes Iranian, Armenian and Sanskrit (the ancient literary language of India), as well as most modern European languages. The name is also given to those groups of people speaking early Indo-European languages who drifted into the Middle East in about 2000BC. They may have originated in the area that stretches from southern Russia to central Europe.

Israelites. The Hebrew† inhabitants of the Kingdom of **Israel**.

Jews. Another name for the Semitic† people also known as Israelites† and Hebrews†; people who practice the religion **Judaism**.

Medjay. The name of a Nubian tribe some of whose members came to Egypt as mercenary† soldiers. The role of the Medjay later evolved into that of a peace-keeping force, and the term was also applied to native Egyptians who joined it.

Mercenary. A man who fights for pay in a foreign army.

Miracle. A wonderful event which cannot be explained by natural causes and is attributed to divine intervention.

Mummy. An embalmed body ready for burial.

Necropolis. A cemetery.

Next World. The place where the Egyptians thought people lived after death.

Nomads. People who do not live permanently in any one area, but move from place to place. People who live in this way are described as **nomadic**.

Nome. The Greek name for an Egyptian administrative district. Each *nome* was governed by an official called a **nomarch**.

Oracle. A message from a god or goddess. In Egypt it was usually communicated through a cult statue or a sacred animal, in response to questions posed by priests on behalf of worshippers. People consulted the oracle in order to find solutions to personal problems and fears. Kings also used it in an attempt to acquire divine approval for their policies.

Ostraca (Singular: **ostracon**). Pieces of broken pottery or stone, used for drawing or writing on.

Overlord. A supreme lord or ruler, who has power over other, lesser rulers.

Papyrus. A reed used to make a form of writing material (also known as papyrus). It was cut into strips which were pressed and dried to make a smooth writing surface.

Patron. Someone who sponsors or helps another person, usually by providing money or a job.

Phrygians. An Indo-European† people from Phrygia, an ancient kingdom in Asia Minor.

Regent. Someone who rules in the place of the actual ruler who is either absent, incapable or, more commonly, still too young to take power.

Relief. A sculpture carved on a flat background. Raised reliefs were made by cutting away the background and modelling details on to the figures. Sunken reliefs were made by cutting away stone from inside the outlines of the figures and carving the details out of the body.

Romans. A people from the city of Rome in central Italy, founded in the 8th century BC, which became the centre of a great civilization. The Romans built up a huge empire in Europe and around the Mediterranean, conquering Egypt in 30BC. Their empire reached its greatest extent in the 1st century AD and declined in the 4th century AD, but its cultural influence continues to the present day.

Sacrifice. A gift or offering made to a deity by people of early civilizations. This sometimes consisted of fruit, vegetables or flowers, but it could also involve the ritual killing of animals and humans.

Scribe. A person specifically employed to write and copy texts and keep records. This was a highly regarded profession in the ancient times, when relatively few people could read and write. Scribes were eligible for well-paid and prestigious jobs in government.

Second Cataract. See **Cataract**. The frontier between Egypt and Nubia in the Middle Kingdom. The site of the great Middle Kingdom fortresses.

Seleucid. A dynasty and kingdom founded by Seleucus Nicator, a Macedonian general under Alexander the Great†. In 304BC the Seleucids seized a large part of Alexander's empire, but it proved impossible to hold together. Large areas began to break away. In 64BC Seleucid lands were conquered by the Romans† and incorporated into the Roman empire.

Semites. Groups of peoples who, in about 2500BC, occupied an area which stretched from northern Mesopotamia to the eastern borders of Egypt. The Semites spoke closely related dialects which form part of the language group known by modern scholars as **Semitic**. Early Semites include the Akkadians and the Babylonians. Jews† and Arabs† are modern Semites.

Shrine. This is both a temple where a deity is worshipped and a container of wood, stone or precious metal in which the figure of a god or goddess is kept.

Shroud. A reactangular piece of cloth used to enclose a dead body.

Sphinx. In Egypt, statue representing the sun god. A sphinx usually had the body of an animal with the head of a lion, ram or pharaoh.

Stela (plural: **stelae**). An upright reactangular stone slab (sometimes curved at the top), carved with inscriptions. *Stelae* were used to commemorate special events and were also put in tombs to record the names and titles of the dead person and his or her family.

Terracotta. A mixture of clay and sand, used to make tiles and small statues. The statues themselves are sometimes called terracottas.

Tribute. A payment in money or kind made by a ruler or state to another, as an acknowledgement of submission. A vassal† pays tribute to an overlord†.

Underworld. Another name for the Next World†, the kindom of the god Osiris, ruler of the dead. The Egyptians sometimes referred to it as the Kingdom of the West, because it was thought to be somewhere in the far west.

Date chart

This chart lists the most important dates in the history of the early civilizations discussed in this book. It also includes some dates relating to the civilizations of Greece and Rome, which developed within the same period.

From c.10,000BC   Farming develops in the Fertile Crescent.

c.8000BC   Early town is established at Jericho.

Before c.6000BC   Early town is established at Çatal Hüyük.

c.5000BC   Ubaid culture in Sumer.

c.5000BC   Yangshao culture in China; farming settlements are established by the Huang Ho River.

c.5000-3100BC   Predynastic Period in Egypt.

c.4000BC   Uruk culture in Sumer.

c.3500BC   Writing develops in Sumer. Sumerians also invent the wheel and learn how to make bronze.

c.3300-3100BC   Hieroglyphic writing develops in Egypt.

c.3100BC   Egypt is united by Menes.

c.3100-2649BC   Archaic Period in Egypt.

c.3000-2000BC   Independent city states flourish in Sumer, Akkad and Canaan. Early Bronze Age in Canaan.

c.3000-1500BC   Indus Valley Civilization in India.

c.3000-1100BC   Bronze Age in Greece.

c.2900-2400BC   Early dynasties develop in Sumer.

c.2649-2150BC   The Old Kingdom in Egypt; the pyramids are built.

c.2590BC   Pyramid of Cheops (the Great Pyramid of Gizah) is built.

c.2500BC   Longshan culture in China.

c.2500-1500BC   Stonehenge is built in Britain.

c.2371BC   Sargon of Akkad seizes the throne of the city of Kish and builds up an empire in Mesopotamia.

c.2205-1766BC   Traditional dates for legendary Hsia (Xia) Dynasty in China.

c.2150-2040BC   First Intermediate Period in Egypt.

c.2100-2000BC   Dynasty III of Ur.

c.2040-1640BC   The Middle Kingdom in Egypt.

c.2000BC   Amorites conquer Mesopotamia and Assyria and set up independent city states in Canaan. Indo-Europeans drift into the Middle East.

By c.2000BC   There is a flourishing civilization on Crete.

c.2000-1500BC   Middle Bronze Age in Canaan.

c.2000-1450BC   The Old Assyrian Empire.

c.2000-1000BC   Hurrians form an aristocratic caste in many cities in Canaan, ruling the Amorites and native Canaanites.

c.1900BC   Palaces are built on Crete.

c.1813-1781BC   Reign of Shamshi-Adad of Assyria. He builds up an empire from Mari to Babylon.

c.1792-1750BC   Reign of Hammurabi of Babylon.

1766-1027BC   Shang Dynasty in China.

c.1740BC   Hittites are united under one kingdom.

c.1700BC   Cretan palaces are destroyed by earthquakes and then rebuilt.

c.1674BC   Nile Delta is overrun with Hyksos, a people from the Middle East.

c.1640-1552BC   The Second Intermediate Period in Egypt.

c.1600BC   Rise of the Mycenaean culture in Greece.

1552-1069BC   The New Kingdom in Egypt; the greatest period of the Egyptian empire. Royal tombs are built in the Valley of the Kings.

c.1500BC   Groups of Indo-Europeans known as Aryans arrive in India.

c.1500BC   Mitannians unite the Hurrian kingdoms under their rule.

c.1595BC   Hittites plunder Babylon and destroy the Amorite kingdom.

c.1570-1158BC   Kassite dynasty rules in Babylon.

c.1550-1150BC   Late Bronze Age in Canaan.

c.1500BC   Aryans settle in Persia.

c.1500BC   Writing develops in China.

c.1500BC   Decline of the Indus Valley Civilization in India.

c.1500-600BC   The Vedic Period in India; the Hindu religion is gradually established.

1490-1436BC   Reign of Tuthmosis III in Egypt; the greatest of the warrior pharaohs.

c.1450BC   Minoan civilization comes to an end. Palaces are destroyed and Crete is taken over by Mycenaeans.

c.1450-1390BC   Mitannians conquer Assyria and build an empire from the Zagros mountains to the Mediterranean.

c.1450-1200BC   Hittite New Kingdom.

1440BC   Mitannians make a peace treaty with the Egyptians.

1380BC   Accession of Shuppiluliuma, one of the greatest Hittite kings. He overthrows the Mitannian empire and captures northern provinces of the Egyptian empire (Syria).

1364-1347BC   Reign of Akhenaten (Amenhotep IV) in Egypt.

1363-1000BC   The Middle Assyrian Empire.

1289-1224BC   Reign of Ramesses II in Egypt; a great warrior and a prolific builder.

c.1200BC   The advance of the Sea Peoples, raiders and settlers from Greece and the Mediterranean islands.

c.1200BC   Decline of Mycenaean culture in Greece.

1196BC Sea Peoples destroy the Hittite empire. Some Hittite survivors establish small Neo-Hittite states.

1184-1153BC Reign of Ramesses III; the last great warrior pharaoh. He defeats the Sea Peoples.

c.1158BC Kassite rulers are thrown out of Babylon. After an unsettled period Babylonian rule is restored.

c.1100BC Phoenicians are established in coastal cities of Canaan. They found colonies around the southern and western shores of the Mediterranean, with leading cities at Byblos, Sidon, Beirut and Tyre.

1069-664BC Third Intermediate Period in Egypt.

c.1030-1010BC Reign of Saul, first King of the Israelites.

1027-221BC Chou (Zhou) Dynasty in China.

c.1000-612BC The New Assyrian Empire; the greatest period of conquest and expansion.

c.970-930BC Reign of King Solomon of the Israelites. Israelite power reaches its height.

c.900BC The *Rig Veda* is composed in India.

c.814BC Phoenicians found the city of Carthage on the North African coast.

c.800-500BC The Archaic Period in Greece; a Greek alphabet is introduced, the first Olympic Games is held and the poet Homer composes the *Iliad* and the *Odyssey* (tales of the Trojan wars).

c.753BC Traditional date for the founding of Rome.

728BC Egypt is conquered by Piankhi, a Nubian king.

726-722BC Reign of Shalmaneser V of Assyria who conquers the Kingdom of Israel.

c.722-481BC Spring and Autumn Period in China; small states fight each other for supremacy.

721-705BC Reign of Sargon II of Assyria.

c.700BC Achaemenid Dynasty established in Persia.

c.670BC Kingdom of Medea established.

664-525BC The Late Period in Egypt begins with the Saite Dynasty; Egyptian independence is restored.

668-627BC Reign of Ashurbanipal II of Assyria; he sacks Thebes (Egypt), Babylon and Susa (Persia).

c.650BC The first coins are introduced in Lydia.

626-539BC The New Babylonian Empire.

612BC Ashur and Nineveh fall to the Medes and Babylonians.

605-562BC Reign of Nebuchadnezzar II of Babylon.

c.600-500BC Nubians abandon their capital at Napata and move south to Meroë

c.600BC Introduction of Taoism in China by the prophet Lao-zi.

597BC The Babylonian Captivity; Nebuchadnezzar II occupies Jerusalem and carries off many of its leading citizens to Babylon. After a further revolt in 587-586BC he sacks Jerusalem and again deports many of the people to Babylon.

c.560-483BC The life of the Buddha.

551-479BC Life of Kong zi (also known as Confucius), Chinese philosopher and prophet.

c.550BC Medea and Persia are united by Cyrus II. He conquers Lydia and the Babylonian empire.

525BC Cambyses II of Persia conquers Egypt.

c.510BC Rome becomes a republic.

c.500-336BC The Classical Period in Greece; the great age of Greek civilization.

490-449BC Wars between Greece and Persia.

c.481-221BC Warring States Period in China; seven major states destroy each other in struggles for power.

c.465BC Persian empire is in decline.

404-343BC Egyptians overthrow their Persian rulers and set up native dynasties.

343-332BC Persians retake Egypt.

334-331BC Alexander the Great of Macedonia conquers the Persian empire. He is accepted by the Egyptians as pharaoh.

331BC Alexandria becomes the new capital of Egypt.

323BC Alexander the Great dies and Egypt comes under the control of General Ptolemy.

323-281BC Wars of the Diadochi.

305-30BC Ptolemaic Dynasty in Egypt.

301-64BC The Seleucid Dynasty rules an empire in Asia Minor.

c.300-200BC Alphabetic script is developed in Meroë.

280-268BC The Antigonid Dynasty rules in Macedonia.

c.272-231BC Asoka of the Maurya Dynasty unites most of India under his rule.

264BC Rome now dominates the whole of Italy.

264-241BC First Punic War between the Romans and the Carthaginians.

221BC Unification of China by the first Ch'in emperor, Shi-huang-ti.

218-202BC Second Punic War.

214BC The Great Wall of China is built to keep out hostile tribes, the Hsiung-Nu (also known as Huns).

206BC-AD222 Han Dynasty rules China.

149-146BC Third Punic War ends with the destruction of Carthage.

133-31BC The Romans expand throughout the Mediterranean and build up a huge empire.

c.100BC Paper is invented in China.

51-30BC Reign of Queen Cleopatra VII of Egypt.

31BC Anthony and Cleopatra are defeated by the Romans at the Battle of Actium.

30BC Egypt becomes a province of the Roman empire.

Index

First published in 1991 by Usborne Publishing Ltd,
Usborne House, 83-85 Saffron Hill, London EC1N 8RT, England.

Printed in Great Britain